Journal for Distinguished Language Studies

Volume 8

Copyright 2022

The purpose of the *Journal for Distinguished Language Studies* (ISSN 1547-7819) is to provide a forum for exchanging information about teaching to and reaching near-native foreign language proficiency for teachers, learners, and professional language users. Areas of interest include research, theory, and practical application.

The *Journal for Distinguished Language Studies* was published annually from 2003-2010 by the Coalition of Distinguished Language Studies, which closed in 2010. In 2020, editorship of the JDLS passed to MSI Press LLC. A bridge volume (Volume 7: 2011-2020) was published in late 2020. The current issues are published bi-annually in even years by MSI Press LLC in Hollister, California. Subscriptions are available and can be facilitated through orders@msipress.com or by fax/phone, 831-886-2486.

Prospective contributors should contact one of the editors, Dr. Yalun Zhou (zhouy12@rpi.edu) or Dr. Donna Bain Butler (dbutler@desu.edu).

ISBN 9781950328856

ISSN 1547-7819

Copyright 2022

All rights reserved. No part of this journal may be reproduced in any form without permission of the publisher, except in the case of brief quotations embedded in critical articles and reviews or material already in the public domain.

The editors and publisher assume no responsibility for statements of fact or opinion by the authors.

EDITORIAL STAFF

- Editor, Dr. Yalun Zhou, Rensselaer Polytechnic Institute, New York, USA
- Associate Editor, Dr. Donna Bain Butler, Delaware State University, Delaware, USA

ADVISORY BOARD

- Dr. Rajai Al-Khanji, University of Jordan
- Dr. Andrew Corin, Defense Language Institute (Emeritus)
- Dr. Rebecca Oxford, University of Alabama at Birmingham
- Dr. Karin Ryding, Georgetown University (Emerita)
- Dr. Nelleke Van Deusen-Scholle, Yale University

FRIENDS OF DISTINGUISHED LANGUAGE PROFICIENCY

2003. Ambassador Ruth Davis
2004. Dr. Dan Davidson & Dr. Maria Lekic
2005. HRH Firas bin Raad of Jordan & Renee Meyer
2006. Dr. Richard Brecht
2007. Ambassador James Collins
2008. Kevin Gormley
2009. Dina Kupchanka
2010. Boris Shekhtman & Dr. Betty Lou Leaver
2011-2020. Dr. Madeline Ehrman & Dr. Ray Clifford
2021-2022. Dr. Christine Campbell & Dr. David Wilmsen

To nominate a candidate for the 2023-2024 Friend of Distinguished Language Proficiency Award, send a short justification related to Level 4 contribution(s) and, if available, a CV to the JDLS editors.

EDITORIAL MAILING OFFICE
Journal for Distinguished Language Studies
c/o MSI Press LLC
1760-F Airline Hwy, #203
Hollister, CA 95023

Table of Contents

EDITORS' NOTE 1

FRIEND OF DISTINGUISHED LANGUAGE PROFICIENCY AWARD 3

PERSONAL EXPERIENCE 7

How I Attained "Near-Native" Proficiency in Chinese (Cornelius C. Kubler) 9

FEATURE ARTICLES 21

Beyond the Language: Debating as High-Intensity Cultural Engagement & Leadership (Emilie Cleret) 23

Helping Learners Achieve the Distinguished Level of Proficiency (James E. Bernhardt) 37

Roadmaps to Distinguished Speaking Proficiency (Jack Franke) 53

On the Cusp: Zone of Proximal Development Tables to Guide Formative Assessment (Betty Lou Leaver) 69

Protocol-Based Formative Assessment: Evolution and Revolution at the Defense Language Institute Foreign Language Center (Andrew R. Corin & Sergey Entis) 95

ABSTRACTS 117

Abstracts in Chinese 119

Abstracts in English 123

Abstracts in French 127

Abstracts in German 131

Abstracts in Russian 135

Abstracts in Spanish 139

BOOK REVIEWS 143

Lessons from Exceptional Language Learners Who Have Achieved Native like Proficiency: Motivation, Cognition, and Identity (reviewed by Natalia Lord) 145

Mastering Italian through Global Debate by Marie Bertola and Sandra Carletti (reviewed by Alessandra Rice and Francesca Gasparella) 147

Mastering Spanish through Global Debate by Nieves Pérez Knapp, Krishuana Hines-Gaither, and Morella Ruscitti-Tovar (reviewed by Joseph Fees). 150

Practices That Work: Bringing Learners to Professional Proficiency in World Languages Editor, edited by Thomas Jesús Garza (reviewed by Michael Wei) . . 153

Stories from Exceptional Language Learners Who Have Achieved Nativelike Proficiency by Katarina Mentzelopoulos and Zoltán Dörnyei with Capucine Trotignon (reviewed by Thomas Jesús Garza) 156

IN MEMORIAM 159

Professor Zoltán Dörnyei June 10, 2022. 161

Carl D. Leaver 1948-2021 163

LIST OF CONTRIBUTORS TO THIS VOLUME. 165

CALL FOR PAPERS 167

EDITORS' NOTE

The *Journal for Distinguished Language Studies* (JDLS) is a refereed volume published in 2003 by the Coalition of Distinguished Language Centers (founded in 2002) under the direction of Dr. Betty Lou Leaver and Boris Shekhtman. After transitioning to a new publisher, MSI Press LLC, JDLS has published a bridge issue (Issue 7) covering the years 2011-2020 when the journal was on hiatus as a result of the previous publisher experiencing difficulty in funding publication. Following the bridge issue, the JDLS now moves to regular biennial publication.

JDLS is the only journal to focus exclusively on the highest levels of language achievement: that is, native-like or near-native. This level is labeled "distinguished" by the American Council on the Teaching of Foreign Languages (ACTFL) and "Level 4/advanced professional proficiency" by the Interagency Language Roundtable (ILR). Descriptions can be found on the ACTFL and ILR websites.

The purpose of the journal is to create a robust international movement to promote language learning to the near-native level of proficiency. The editors seek contributions in the areas of theory, research (quantitative, qualitative, case studies, action research), and applications. The journal typically has published a balance of articles in all three categories. Published papers develop theory, share applications that work (based on the experience of those who teach that level), and report on the research needed for proper evaluation and assessment of theory and application.

The editors particularly welcome articles on the following areas:

- current status of Level 4 proficiency research in each of the four skill areas;
- teaching methods to/at/above Level 4 proficiency in each of the four skill areas;
- the role of culture in achieving Level 4 proficiency in each of the four skill areas; and
- assessment to/at/above Level 4 proficiency in each of the four skill areas.

The articles published here represent original work. They have not been previously published elsewhere or submitted to another journal or collected volume. The editors welcome questions or input at any time.

- **Editor**, Yalun Zhou, Ph.D., Rensselaer Polytechnic Institute, New York, USA
- **Associate Editor**, Donna Bain Butler, Ph.D., Delaware State University, Delaware, USA

Issue 8 contains five research articles, one superior language learner personal story, five book reviews, and two memorials dedicated to outstanding Level 4 contributors: Carl Leaver (publishing support) and Zoltán Dörnyei (L2 research, theory, and practice). Among the five research articles, Cleret explores how debating is used in senior professional military education at the French War College in Paris to help officers attain native-live English language competence. Bernhardt suggests that learners aiming to achieve distinguished levels of proficiency should focus on expanding their vocabulary and advocates for instructional designs that provide extensive input through reading, listening, and watching. He emphasizes the importance of evaluating materials based on vocabulary and individual learner needs, rejecting standardized proficiency goals, and promoting learner-centered approaches to instruction. Franke's article explores the role of persistence, study abroad, motivation, and learner autonomy in the pursuit of distinguished speaking proficiency in foreign languages, emphasizing the personal nature of this pursuit and highlighting the importance of engagement in the target culture and extended immersion experiences. Leaver discusses the significant gap between proficiency levels in language learning and the development of cusp tables to identify critical proficiency elements for advancing from one level to another, utilizing formative assessment and learners' zone of proximal development to determine personalized next steps. Corin and Entis provide examples of formative assessment in practice for learning and instruction at upper levels of proficiency.

In addition to the five research articles, Kubler's personal story recounts his unexpected journey of majoring in Chinese, achieving high proficiency levels, and using Chinese as his primary professional language in both government and academic careers. Lord reviews the book *Lessons from Exceptional Language Learners Who Have Achieved Nativelike Proficiency: Motivation, Cognition and Identity* (Dörnyei & Mentzelopoulos, 2022); Garza reviews Dörnyei and collaborators' other book, *Stories from Exceptional Language Learners Who Have Achieved Nativelike Proficiency* (Mentzelopoulos, Dörnyei, and Trotignon, 2023), showcasing the personal narratives of thirty diverse learners who have achieved remarkable nativelike proficiency through different motivations and paths. Rice reviews the book, *Mastering Italian Through Global Debate* (Bertola & Carletti, 2022), introducing the pedagogical approach of global debate to achieve Level-4 proficiency and assessment criteria. Fees reviews the book, *Mastering Spanish through Global Debate* (Knapp, Hines-Gaither, and Ruscitti-Tovar, 2022), designed to develop advanced Spanish skills aligned with the Superior level proficiency set by ACTFL. Last, Wei reviews *Practices that Works: Bring Learners to Professional Proficiency in World Languages* (Garza, 2021), an update of the book, *What Works*, published by the Coalition of Distinguished Language Centers in 2008, aiming to demonstrate the achievability of professional proficiency, providing guidance on how to attain these results, and emphasizing the importance of including world language education in every educational curriculum and individual's awareness.

Dr. Yalun Zhou, Rensselaer Polytechnical University
Dr. Donna Bain Butler, Delaware State University

FRIEND OF DISTINGUISHED LANGUAGE PROFICIENCY AWARD

The Coalition of Distinguished Language Centers, which established the *Journal for Distinguished Language Proficiency*, presented an annual Friend of Distinguished Language Proficiency award to individuals who had significantly contributed to the mission of the journal of promoting the acquisition of native-like second-language proficiency. With its acquisition of the journal in 2020, MSI Press LLC, with the guidance of the JDLS advisory board, has continued the award. Recipients of the award to date are listed in the JDLS masthead.

Anyone may recommend an individual to be considered for the award by contacting one of the journal editors or advisors with a description of the ways in which the individual has promoted distinguished language proficiency through service, career, publication, or in other ways or a combination thereof.

The following "friends of distinguished language proficiency" have been selected in the recent competitions. For this volume, they were asked to provide biographical statements that they would like to share with readers.

2011-2020

Dr. Ray Clifford

Ray Clifford's career has included both government and academic assignments, and in both of those venues he has sought to promote the value of high-level language proficiency. His research includes exploring the relationship between superior language proficiency and cognitive development, the acquisition of language in non-traditional settings, and the advantages of using criterion-referenced tests to assess individuals' language proficiency. While Chancellor of the Defense Language Institute Foreign Language Center, he instituted a classification system for language jobs that replaced the traditional focus on the frequency of the communication tasks encountered with an emphasis on the infrequent, but critical communication tasks that required nuanced, accurate communications. At Brigham Young University, he instituted a university-wide language certification program that is based on students' tested proficiency rather than on the number of classes they have taken. In all his assignments, he has demonstrated that the measurement of language proficiency is an essential component of instructional program management.

Dr. Madeline Ehrman

(posthumous biographical statement prepared by Betty Lou Leaver)

For many years, Madeline Ehrman served as Director of Research, Evaluation, and Development at the School of Language Studies, Foreign Service Institute of the U. S. Department of State, a division which she helped co-found. She headed a staff responsible for institutional research, staff and program development, language proficiency testing, and learning style consultations for incoming students and those having special difficulties. Prior to that, she served as acting associate dean, as chair of the Asian and African languages department, and regional language training supervisor in Bangkok. More recently, she concurrently served as an associate at the National Foreign Language Center and as an associate at the Center for the Advanced Study of Language. Her Ph.D. in clinical psychology was followed by training in psychoanalytic psychotherapy at the Washington School of Psychiatry. She co-developed the E&L Cognitive Styles Construct, a learning styles identification instrument in use at a number of institutions in several countries plus in U. S. government language programs. She has published a number of textbooks for Southeast Asian languages, multiple articles and book chapters on language learning topics and interpersonal relations, and four books: *Achieving Success in Second Language Acquisition* (with Betty Lou Leaver and Boris Shekhtman, Cambridge University Press), *Interpersonal Dynamics in Second Language Education: The Visible and Invisible Classroom* (with Zoltan Dörnyei, Sage), *The Meanings of the Modals in Present-Day American English*, and *Understanding Second Language Learning Difficulties* (Sage). She spoke a number of languages, including Thai and Cambodian, having worked with Indochinese refugee operations. Madeline succumbed to cancer in October 2015. Following her death, the U. S. Department of State established the Madeline E. Ehrman Fellowship in Second Language Acquisition for scholars whose work addresses efficient and effective second language training for adults.

2021-2022

Dr. Christine Campbell

Christine Campbell is President, Campbell Language Consultants and was Teacher, Department Chair, Dean, Assistant Provost, and Associate Provost at the Defense Language Institute Foreign Language Center (DLIFLC) for 30 years. In her last position at DLIFLC, she headed a directorate that practiced transformative teaching and learning. Her recent publications, in edited volumes, have focused on this topic, including a co-edited award-winning volume, *Transformative Language Learning and Teaching* and a forthcoming co-edited volume, *Open Architecture Curricular Design*.

Dr. David Wilsem

Arabic presents especial challenges to students aiming to acquire native-like proficiency with it. By now, the reasons for that are known: Arabic has diglossia. That is, its spoken varieties are in some ways strikingly different from its written form. If that is not challenging enough for learners of the language, the challenge is compounded by the near universal practice in Arabic-language programs, requiring students to begin their study with the written form of the language, which is not usually declaimed aloud in everyday conversation, before providing them with some instruction in a spoken variety, usually a semester or, with luck, two. Some programs provide no instruction in spoken Arabic at all! I like to say that such an approach is like teaching students to fly before they learn to walk! Given that, my experience in learning Arabic was atypical. I began my study at the University of Arizona with an intensive summer program in a Gulf Arabic dialect before continuing to tackle the intricacies of Arabic writing. The program at Arizona is, even to this day, unusual for its providing instruction in no fewer than three regional dialects of Arabic, with one of them, four full semesters. I was fortunate to spend my second summer with the language in an intensive study-abroad program at Yarmouk University in Irbid, Jordan, a partnership between that university and the University of Virginia. I returned to the fall semester at my home institution far ahead of my classmates in my facility with both the spoken and written varieties of the language. Soon after that, I joined the intensive year-long program at the Center for Arabic Study Abroad (CASA) at the American University of Cairo. I distinctly recall the moment when I recognized that I had achieved full functional proficiency. A few months into intensive study, I was stopped on the street by someone who asked me for directions. I answered in Egyptian Arabic without hesitation, giving detailed instructions. As the scene dissolved, I said to myself, "I've got it!" Because of my experience with learning spoken Arabic first and enjoying the opportunity to study the language in its natural environments, I developed a strong belief in the imperative of learning a spoken form of the language first – the so-called 'colloquial-first' approach, which remains a minority stance in the Arabic-teaching profession – and in the efficacy of study-abroad. For that reason, I have spent my career teaching in and directing Arabic study-abroad programs, emphasizing the local dialects. To be sure, living in the Arab world for thirty years, teaching at American universities in Cairo, Beirut, and Sharjah, has enhanced my proficiency, but those gains have been incremental, building upon my fastest and most profound achievements in attaining native-like proficiency in Arabic, which came in my early years with the language. In closing, I should repeat what I tell all students in the orientation sessions with which they begin their intensive study-abroad: I began my road to native-like proficiency with Arabic in graduate school at the age of thirty-one. If I can do it, others surely can!

PERSONAL EXPERIENCE

How I Attained "Near-Native" Proficiency in Chinese

Cornelius C. Kubler (Williams College, USA)

The Beginning

I grew up in a German-speaking family in Daytona Beach, Florida and studied Spanish, French, and Latin in junior and senior high school as well as a little Italian and Esperanto at the local YWCA. Thus, foreign languages – specifically, European languages – have been an important part of my life since childhood. However, never in the world would I have imagined that I would end up majoring in Chinese and linguistics in college, test twice in Chinese at the ILR S-4/R-4 level in the civil and foreign service of the U.S. State Department, and use Chinese as my primary professional language throughout my two careers as State Department official and college professor.

What happened? Well, the summer before my freshman year at Cornell University, I traveled to Ithaca, New York for a special six-week program in Attic Greek and French existentialist thought. Through pure serendipity, I was assigned as roommate to a Chinese-American fellow from Brooklyn, New York. I quickly became good friends with David, who would sometimes teach me a few words of spoken Mandarin, demonstrate how Chinese characters worked (日 **rì** "sun" + 月 **yuè** "moon" → 明 **míng** "bright"), and regale me with stories of his childhood in Taipei. When I was hungry, he would invite me to taste dried cuttlefish, pineapple cakes, and other snacks his mother periodically sent from New York City Chinatown; and when I was sick, he would offer me 川貝枇杷膏 **Chuānbèi Pípa Gāo** "Sichuan fritillaria and loquat syrup" from his traditional Chinese medicine kit that his mother had packed in his suitcase before he left for college.

When the time for fall term course registration arrived, I decided—because of David's influence but against the advice of one of my professors—to drop Greek and instead take Chinese 101, which would have the added benefit of satisfying the requirement for the linguistics major of one semester of a non-European language. In truth, my intention was to take a semester of Chinese and then turn my attention back to European languages and linguistics. But that plan would turn out very differently.

Learning Chinese at Cornell University

I quickly got hooked on Chinese. I found Chinese fascinating in how it differed from the Indo-European languages with which I was familiar: no noun declensions or verb conjugations, no tenses, no obligatory singular or plural distinction for nouns, a classifier for every noun, and adjectives and prepositions that were really verbs! Knowing German and French helped me with some of the sounds of Mandarin, for example, the vowel **ü** as in 綠 **lǜ** "be green", which is like the **ü** of German **Tür** "door" or the **u** of French **tu** "you (familiar)." My having a good ear for sounds facilitated acquiring the four tones of Mandarin, which I didn't find so very difficult, except that when learning the pronunciation of each new vocabulary word, I had to learn not only the correct consonants and vowels but also remember the proper tone.

When we began learning how to read and write, I found Chinese characters fascinating but hard; I think my auditory memory is better than my visual memory. It took me what seemed like forever to remember all the strokes of relatively basic characters like 壞 **huài** "be bad" (19 strokes) and 讓 **ràng** "let" (24 strokes). I would first write out each character 20 to 30 times and then test myself by covering up the Chinese in the vocabulary list: Could I write the character correctly from memory by looking at the English meaning? At first it would take me two to three hours to memorize 10 characters, though this gradually got a little easier as I became more familiar with the various components of Chinese characters, which often repeat themselves in new permutations.

First-year Chinese was very well taught at Cornell. The curriculum our professor, Nicholas C. Bodman, had devised was highly effective, emphasizing a strong foundation in spoken Chinese for most of the first semester before introducing the elements of the Chinese writing system and practicing the skills of reading and writing several months later. Professor Bodman taught three hours of "lecture" a week, where he would explain Chinese pronunciation, grammar, vocabulary, and culture to us in English from the perspective of the non-native learner; two native-speaking lecturers, Mrs. Ni and Mrs. Wang, who were stellar pedagogues with warm, supportive personalities, taught drill class five hours per week, during which they emphasized accurate pronunciation and grammar and practiced communicative skills with us. This model, now often referred to as "fact class" coupled with the even more important "act class," is a model I have tried to follow all my life in learning and, later, teaching and supervising various languages.

The textbooks we used, from the well-known "Yale Chinese Language Series," were all accompanied by open-reel tape recordings, which I drilled with intensively in the Cornell language laboratory for at least 1-2 hours every day. During my seven years in residence at Cornell, I spent literally hundreds of hours in the language lab, reveling in repetition drills, substitution drills, and transformation drills in Mandarin, Cantonese, Taiwanese, and Japanese. Even though in certain circles today the word "drill" has almost become a dirty word, I am totally convinced that the drill work I did with native-speaker audio recordings played a major role in my linguistic development and is a big part of the reason why I have relatively good pronunciation in these languages for a non-native speaker.

Acquiring Chinese in Taiwan

In the spring of 1971, I learned that I had won a scholarship from Rotary International Foundation to spend a year at National Chengchi University (NCCU) in Taipei, Taiwan as a Rotary Undergraduate Scholar. With good intentions but insufficient understanding of the difficulties for an English speaker in learning Chinese, Rotary stipulated that I must study at a regular Taiwanese university rather than a language school for foreigners, so that I might be able to mix and mingle with local citizens and implement the ideal of citizen-to-citizen international exchange. And so, in September of that year, after having studied Mandarin for only four semesters, I moved to Taipei to begin my freshman year as a student in the Department of Chinese at NCCU. I lived in a clean but spartan dormitory with four Taiwanese and one overseas Chinese roommate from Vietnam and took courses including Freshman Chinese, Chinese General History, Political Thought of Dr. Sun Yat-sen, Ethics, Music, and Physical Education.

Classes at NCCU were almost exclusively lecture style, though a few instructors would address an occasional question to the class as a whole. I didn't realize it then, but this type of instruction resulted in my listening comprehension gradually improving but my having little opportunity to practice speaking about formal, academic topics. Comprehending the accented Mandarin of my instructors proved to be a major challenge. My homeroom teacher, who was also the one who taught us the lecture section of Freshman Chinese, was a younger man from Taiwan with only a moderate Taiwanese accent in his Mandarin, which I could manage. However, the professors in my other classes were mainland émigrés from Sichuan, Jiangsu, and other provinces of mainland China who spoke Mandarin with such heavy local accents that even my Taiwanese classmates would sometimes complain they couldn't understand what their professors were saying! Reading the cursive characters my professors would scribble on the blackboard was another source of difficulty, since in my American university Chinese classes, we had been exposed only to printed-style characters.

That fall semester at NCCU I felt completely overwhelmed, as if I had been thrown into the ocean and was trying to keep my head above water, with one breaker after another crashing against me from all directions. By far the biggest challenges were the semi-classical style in which most of my textbooks were written as well as the quantity of reading involved. I was frantically memorizing huge amounts of Chinese just to pass tests and exams without really understanding what I was memorizing. I would spend many hours each day in the library looking up characters and copying them and their pronunciations and translations into vocabulary notebooks, but without enough time to learn all those good words I was looking up.

Fortunately, my frustrations about my academic progress at NCCU were in large part made up for by the friendships I quickly formed with my roommates and other students on campus. My classmates were warm and supportive, frequently offering to lend me their class notes, correct my Chinese, or explain the meanings of language or customs I didn't understand. My fluency in informal, everyday Chinese improved through the many bull sessions we had, where we would talk about all the typical topics that young people discuss—schoolwork, family, international news, gossip, relationships, and future plans. With my closest friends I would occasionally discuss, in hushed tones, topics which in Taiwan in the early 1970s one had to be discrete in discussing, for example, Communist China and the Taiwan independence movement. As the first semester came to a close, I took stock of my situation and concluded that, as much as I appreciated the friendship of my classmates, to remain at NCCU for the spring semester just wouldn't be an efficient way to continue my study of Chinese.

I had heard of a Jesuit missionary language school in Hsinchu – about two hours south of Taipei – by the name of Chabanel Language Institute. I went to visit, was much impressed by the faculty and facilities and, with the reluctant agreement of Rotary, moved to Hsinchu in January 1972 to continue my studies. Though I missed socializing with my old classmates at NCCU, I partially made up for this by taking some meals in the cafeteria at nearby National Chiao Tung University, where I made several new friends. Over the next few months, I also made several other new friends on the train between Hsinchu and Taipei, where I would still travel occasionally for Rotary meetings or to visit with NCCU friends.

At Chabanel I was fortunate to receive four hours a day of tutorial training including Short Radio Plays, Chinese History, Introduction to Classical Chinese, and Beginning Taiwanese Hokkien. The teaching methods were excellent, strongly influenced by the audio-lingual method. There was a well-equipped language laboratory, where I drilled with audio recordings several hours each day. Many of the teaching materials employed at Chabanel were prepared and published in-house and were impressively high in quality, no doubt at least in part the result of the training in modern linguistics that some of the Jesuit fathers had received.

The high-quality tutorial training I received during my six months at Chabanel had a huge impact on me in a number of ways. First, it helped me consolidate my Mandarin language proficiency at the high-intermediate level and prepared me for graduate studies in Chinese. Second, it was at Chabanel that I was introduced to Classical Chinese, which I was to study for a number of years afterwards and which I have taught frequently with great professional and personal fulfillment. Third, my semester at Chabanel was the first time I had the opportunity to study a non-Mandarin Sinitic language – Taiwanese Hokkien, which whetted my interest in Chinese dialectology, a major focus of my scholarly research but also very useful for the pay-off in comprehending Mandarin spoken with different local accents.

Back at Cornell, Middlebury, and Teaching for the First Time

Since I had a three-year graduate fellowship waiting for me, I decided to return to Cornell to enroll in the graduate program in linguistics. From 1972-1975 I took courses in general linguistics, Chinese linguistics, modern Chinese language, Classical Chinese, Cantonese, and Taiwanese. I also wrote an M.A. thesis on the topic of Europeanized grammar in modern written Chinese, for which I did a great deal of research using primary sources in Chinese. At Cornell I was fortunate to have the opportunity to learn from eminent specialists in Chinese linguistics and literature including my first teacher of Chinese, Professor Bodman, as well as John McCoy, Tsu-Lin Mei, and Harold Shadick. I spent the summer of 1973 at the Middlebury College Chinese School, where I studied Fifth-year Chinese in an intensive immersion format. The best language lab I have ever been in was at Middlebury, where each booth was completely separate in its own soundproofed room with closeable door. I still remember the many hours I spent in that lab, delighting in the sonorant voices of Beijing Mandarin recorded by instructors from the Yale Institute of Far Eastern Languages.

It was also during this period at Cornell that I taught Chinese for the first time, serving as Teaching Assistant for Chinese 101-102, for which I taught the three weekly grammar lectures as well as being responsible for overall course coordination. As Bill Hopkins (2020: 9) so aptly put it in Volume 7 of this journal, "Nothing helps you learn a subject so much as teaching it does." By having to explain Chinese phonetics, grammar, and vocabulary to others, I gained a deeper understanding of the language myself as well as increasing my confidence in using it. However, after three years back in the States, I was hungry for more exposure to Chinese in country. Since it was not yet possible for Americans to study in China in the mid-1970s and since I had had such a positive experience studying in Taiwan during my junior year, I made the difficult decision to leave Cornell with a Master's degree in June 1975 and return to Taiwan.

Second M.A. and Ph.D.

From 1975-78 I studied as a graduate student in the Graduate School of Chinese Literature at National Taiwan University (NTU) for a second M.A. Again I lived in a university dorm but this time, as graduate students, we were only four in the room. I took courses in Chinese literature, intellectual history, syntax, dialectology, and historical linguistics, for all of which I had to do large amounts of reading. However, unlike my earlier undergraduate experience in Taiwan, this time I was prepared, as my listening comprehension of accented Mandarin, writing ability, reading speed, and proficiency in Classical Chinese had all improved.

Under the guidance of the internationally known linguist Ting Pang-Hsin, I wrote my Master's thesis titled 澎湖群島方言調查 **Pénghú Qúndǎo Fāngyán Diàochá** *A Dialect Survey of the Pescadores Archipelago*. The research for that thesis, which I conducted over a period of over two years, was the most adventurous thing I have ever done in my life, since it involved surveying different subdialects of Southern Min at 88 fishing villages on 17 different islands in the Taiwan Strait, some less than one square kilometer in area with a population of only a few hundred speakers.

After receiving my M.A. from NTU in 1978, I returned to Cornell to study Japanese in the well-known FALCON program directed by Eleanor H. Jorden, whose innovative ideas about East Asian language pedagogy were to have a great influence on me in the years to come. Upon the conclusion of twelve months of super-intensive Japanese language training in Ithaca followed by an additional summer in Japan, I pursued one more year of coursework for the Ph.D. in linguistics at Cornell. Even though I still had my dissertation

—on the topic of language contact in Taiwan—to complete, I decided that after so many years in school, it was time to find a job.

Learning Chinese on the Job

My first full-time position was at the U.S. State Department's Foreign Service Institute (FSI), where American foreign service officers and other government personnel are trained in over 70 languages and cultures. At FSI I took advantage of the opportunity to continue learning Chinese on the job, in accordance with the famous saying in the *Analects* of Confucius: 學而時習之不亦說乎? **Xué ér shí xí zhī bú yì yuè hū?** "Is it not a pleasure to learn something and often put it into practice?" My professional Chinese improved substantially during my years as supervisor of FSI Mandarin and Cantonese training from 1980-81 and again from 1988-1991, when I had concurrent responsibilities as chair of the Department of Asian and African Languages. Much of each day I was involved in class observation, teaching, and individual and group meetings with the native-speaking instructors who hailed from all over mainland China, Hong Kong, and Taiwan. I was also deeply involved in materials preparation and testing in Mandarin, Cantonese, and (for part of the time) Japanese at all levels from S/R-0 to S/R-5.

In 1981 FSI sent me back to Taiwan to serve as principal of its field school for advanced Chinese in Taipei, with additional responsibilities for the American Institute in Taiwan Chinese language program and the Consulate General Hong Kong Post Language Program. I was intensely involved for six years in all aspects of student instruction, instructor recruitment and training, and curriculum development, frequently observing classes and evaluating proficiency tests in Mandarin, Cantonese, and Taiwanese at all levels, especially the 2+ to 3+ range. I frequently chaired meetings with faculty and staff and also began giving lectures at local universities. All of this work was most useful in raising and consolidating my proficiency in Chinese for professional purposes.

After eleven extremely busy but exhilarating years at FSI, I was hired in 1991 by Williams College, a highly selective liberal arts college in Williamstown, Massachusetts to serve as chair of their still fairly new Department of Chinese. In my new career as college professor, most of my language teaching was only at the S/R-0 to S/R-2 levels, with the possible exception of Fourth-year Chinese, some of the materials for which ranged up to S/R-3. Therefore, teaching Chinese at the college level didn't contribute much to raising my own proficiency. However, our Chinese faculty meetings were always conducted in the language, which was of some benefit, and I frequently attended professional conferences in Asia, where I made many presentations in Chinese on Chinese and had the opportunity to listen to presentations by native Chinese-speaking colleagues. I also interacted with presenters at Q&A sessions or informally during breaks and dinners. Moreover, for a total of six years while on sabbatical leave from Williams and also during many summers, I served as visiting professor at various universities in China, Hong Kong, and Taiwan, where I taught graduate courses on Chinese linguistics and language pedagogy. Without doubt, these activities also contributed substantially to maintaining and strengthening my own proficiency in the language.

What I Did Right

In my study of Chinese – full-time from 1969 through 1978 and part-time ever since, I think that, sometimes by plan and sometimes just fortuitously – and always with the support of countless numbers of kind and helpful Chinese, Taiwanese, and Americans to whom I am forever indebted, I ended up doing a lot of things right.

I was lucky to have excellent teachers in the Cornell Chinese program who had high standards but were adept at motivating students like me to study hard through their obvious concern for each of us as individuals and their frequent praise and encouragement. They corrected my pronunciation and grammar patterns diligently and were skilled at both conducting drills and facilitating communicative language practice in their classes. It's so important for learners to develop good pronunciation and grammar habits early on, since it's difficult if not impossible to correct entrenched mistakes once they have fossilized.

In my learning of Chinese, I frequently employed both audio and video materials, everything from pronunciation exercises and grammar drills to radio news broadcasts and television soap operas. Based on my experience learning and teaching Chinese over six decades, I have found grammar drills to be an essential step in helping learners attain or approach the ultimate goal of fluent, native-like communicative competence. Drills can help learners improve their pronunciation, internalize the new vocabulary and grammar structures to which they have been introduced, and develop their fluency. At the same time, drills can increase learners' confidence in speaking Chinese.

At Cornell, NCCU, and NTU, I took many courses in Classical Chinese, the standard written language of China for thousands of years, which has strongly influenced modern written and spoken Chinese. Proficiency in Classical Chinese is very useful for raising one's level in written Chinese and even for high-level spoken Chinese, since many ancient quotations and proverbs, as well as Classical Chinese-influenced grammar constructions, are still used frequently in formal speech and constitute precisely the kind of language that is associated with the S/R-3+ and 4 levels. In addition, I took numerous courses on the linguistic structure of Chinese, which made me more sensitive to the complexities of Chinese phonology and syntax, directly or indirectly helping me further strengthen my proficiency. Here I again agree with what Bill Hopkins (2020: 9) wrote about the utility of taking courses on the linguistic structure of the language you're studying.

At Cornell and in Taiwan, I also took many courses on Chinese literature and history, which helped provide important background information that was helpful in making sense of Chinese culture. In Taiwan, I studied several years of Taiwanese Hokkien, and at Cornell I took two years of Cantonese. Knowledge of these Sinitic languages, both of which are related to Mandarin much as the Germanic or Romance languages are related to each other, proved to be of considerable help in improving my listening comprehension of Mandarin spoken with a southern Chinese accent, which one hears frequently. During my first decade of Chinese study, I regularly read Chinese newspapers and engaged in pleasure reading of short stories, novels, mysteries, and books by Chinese authors about their experiences studying abroad in America, all of which contributed toward strengthening my reading comprehension and speed.

University courses can be useful for developing high-level listening, reading, and writing skills, but they don't do much for improving speaking. It's important to be cognizant of the huge difference between the informal conversation of classmates in a dorm (which might be S-2 or 2+) and the formal discourse of educated native speakers delivering a briefing on international news or giving a televised interview on a professional topic (which would be S-5). From my observation of thousands of learners of Chinese as a non-native language, I conclude that most adult learners won't attain high-level speaking proficiency without a long period of formal instruction. You need a strong, experienced teacher to correct you and systematically extend your proficiency range. Even when studying at the university in Taiwan, I still took one to two hours per week of tutorial classes at a language school. What to do in these private lessons? Try to "activize" the material learned passively in the university classes. Deliver briefings, oral reports, and mini-lectures on the subjects taken up in your other classes, or on current international and domestic news or topics of professional interest. Instructors must have high standards and be unrelenting in their criticism; moreover, they shouldn't be satisfied with correct but lower-level speech and must insist that you keep reaching for the next rung of the proficiency ladder.

Spending a sufficient amount of time in country, in frequent and close contact with native speakers in both formal and informal situations, is also essential. I was fortunate to be able to study, work, and travel for a total of 17 years in many parts of Taiwan, China, and Hong Kong, which allowed me to interact on a daily basis with people from all walks of life: from farmers and small business people to diplomats and academicians. This experience was most useful in improving my listening comprehension of different dialects, of which China has many. To acquire true conversational fluency in informal register, you need to create a living situation for yourself where, for at least two or three years, you are interacting closely with native speakers, for example, living in a dorm or apartment, as I did in Taiwan for several years. And to become good at formal register, you need practice in giving briefings, oral reports, talks, and lectures, as I was lucky to have the opportunity to do through my teaching and lecturing.

Due to my bicultural background, I was completely willing and usually able to adapt chameleon-like to my surroundings, which probably made native Chinese speakers feel more comfortable in interacting with me and thus afforded me additional practice and experience in using Chinese. Because I had good pronunciation and a non-threatening, low-key personality, people were willing to make friends with me. Even during periods when I was back in the U.S., many of my Taiwanese and Chinese friends would write me cards and letters; this proved useful in helping me become familiar with Chinese handwriting, including the cursive and semi-cursive forms of characters. Because these written materials were from good friends, I was strongly incentivized to figure out what they were writing me. And, naturally, I wanted to write back to them, which provided good opportunities to practice writing – both in handwriting the individual Chinese characters and in the even more important skill of composition.

My wife, whom I met in Taiwan during my junior year abroad 51 years ago, is a native speaker of Chinese. Since our relationship began in Mandarin, we have become accustomed to conversing in that language most of the time. This has, without doubt, been beneficial for me in maintaining and gradually improving my overall proficiency and I'm thankful to her for putting up with my non-native Mandarin all this time. I have found speaking Chinese as home language can be helpful in developing listening comprehension and informal speaking skills at a broad S-2 or 2+ level, but it doesn't help much in raising one's proficiency in professional vocabulary or formal grammatical and discourse structures at the S-3 level and beyond. Most people imagine if you have a spouse from another country whom you regularly speak to in their native language, you must be extremely fluent in that language, but this is not necessarily true. The truth is that most conversation within the family is at a level no higher, and often lower, than S-2+: mealtime conversation, discussing what clothes to wear, talking about daily schedules, arranging activities for the children, going shopping, and so forth. Pillow talk doesn't regularly rise to the S-4 level!

What I Should Have Done Better

Though I was fortunate in many ways and did a number of things right, I'm also keenly aware of some of my mistakes and personal limitations. For one thing, I have a bit of a reserved personality and, especially when with people I don't know well, tend not to talk so much; but the fact is that, in general, the more you talk, the more fluent you become. Though I'm a reasonably good writer, I don't consider myself particularly articulate in speech in any language. Yet in training learners in different foreign languages for almost 50 years now, I've found that if they're highly articulate in their native language, they're generally more likely to become articulate in any foreign languages they learn, given a suitable learning environment and, of course, the requisite diligence on their part.

Since testing at the higher levels on the ILR proficiency scale requires a certain degree of articulateness, when I myself have been scheduled to take language proficiency tests, I've had to adopt extreme measures by anticipating questions in the days leading up to the test and systematically preparing and practicing answers; and I've had to make almost superhuman efforts by reading large quantities of newspapers and magazines and watching many hours of television news broadcasts, after which I force myself to practice summing up current events, especially the intricacies of U.S.-China-Taiwan relations, in the style of an educated, articulate native speaker. Now, I certainly can't share the following piece of advice with my underage college students, but I've found that drinking one (but definitely not more than one) glass of Merlot about half an hour before the test helps me have greater confidence and produce a greater amount of fluent discourse than otherwise would be the case!

Another impediment standing in the way of my attaining higher proficiency is that I've been so busy for decades with work responsibilities, I now seldom read Chinese for pleasure. Though I regularly read Chinese reports, journals, and books on linguistics and language pedagogy as well as no end of professional and personal emails, cards, and letters, I seldom read short stories, novels, histories, or other books aimed at the general reader. Moreover, as we all know, a good language learner should at all times be a careful observer of society. While I sometimes do that when in Asia, far too often I'm thinking about distant issues and am insufficiently focused on the here and now. This personal trait, which I've found difficult to change, has also been to my disadvantage.

So, have I truly acquired near-native proficiency? On the one hand, I can comfortably, confidently, and (almost always) effectively use Chinese for both daily life activities and the professional purposes that apply to me. I can think and speak in Chinese for hours on end and not seldom find myself dreaming in the language. Over the years, I've interpreted on numerous occasions for ambassadors and other high-level State Department officials, college presidents, and VIPs, including once for former Secretary of State Madeline Albright when she visited China. I've often participated in and not infrequently chaired meetings in Chinese, and I frequently deliver lectures, teach graduate seminars, and take part in M.A. and Ph.D. thesis defenses at Chinese and Taiwanese universities. Still, sometimes I wonder what "near native" really means; perhaps I'm really only a rather broad and fluent S-3+ most of the time?

Conclusion

Though I would never have thought when I was growing up that I would spend most of my professional life so closely involved with Chinese language, society, and culture, in looking back as I approach retirement sometime in the next few years, I'm grateful to have had the opportunities I've had. I know that my proficiency in Chinese – and the friends it has enabled me to make, the fascinating people it has allowed me to meet, the places it has allowed me to visit, and the experiences it has allowed me to have –have made my life richer and more interesting and have helped me make a modest contribution to American society and the societies of the Chinese-speaking countries. And, by Jove, I'm not quite done yet!

Reference

Hopkins, Bill. (2020). How I achieved near native fluency in Russian. *Journal for Distinguished Language Studies* 7 (pp. 5-13). Hollister, CA: MSI Press LLC.

About the Author

Cornelius C. Kubler is Stanfield Professor of Asian Studies at Williams College, where he for many years chaired the Department of Asian Studies. He is concurrently adjunct University Chair Professor at National Chengchi University in Taipei and has served as Visiting Professor at National Taiwan Normal University, National Tsing Hua University, and Chinese University of Hong Kong. He served from 2014-16 as Co-Director of the Johns Hopkins University-Nanjing University Center for Chinese and American Studies in Nanjing and has directed Chinese language training programs in the U.S., China, and Taiwan. Previously he was Mandarin, Cantonese, and Japanese Language Training Supervisor and Chair of the Department of Asian & African Languages at the Foreign Service Institute, U.S. Department of State, and served for 6 years as Principal of the AIT Chinese Language & Area Studies School in Taipei. He is principal author of the new *Basic Mandarin Chinese* series and has published over 60 articles and 33 books on Chinese language pedagogy and linguistics.

FEATURE ARTICLES

Beyond the Language:
Debating as High-Intensity Cultural Engagement & Leadership

Emilie Cleret, French War College (France)

Abstract

This article discusses the use of debating in senior Professional Military Education (PME) at the French War College in Paris to help officers reach native-like English language competence.

In France, senior Professional Military Education (PME) is delivered by two schools – Ecole de Guerre (French War College) and Centre des hautes études militaires, (Centre for Higher Military Studies). This article explores the use of debating by the English Studies Department to support the officers' effort to achieve a native-like level of second language (L2) competence during their one-year course in the French War College. The author's perspective is that of a practitioner who heads this department, designs the courses, and manages the faculty that delivers them. All the members of the faculty are from English-speaking countries.

Keywords: Debating, Leadership, (French) Military Education, Culture, Argumentation, Public Speaking

The French War College: Background and Student Body

Ecole de Guerre is located in the eighteenth-century heritage buildings of Ecole Militaire, opposite the Eiffel Tower, in the heart of Paris. Every year, a new intake is selected by a competitive exam that is open to officers from the three services – Army, Navy, Air Force, the Gendarmerie, and the support branches. These 200 French officers are also joined by 100 international officers and 50 civilian attendees. The French officers have 15-20 years of experience in the field on all five continents in all types of operations.

In the second part of their career, their interactions with counterparts from the United States of America, the United Kingdom, and Australia, key English-speaking allies, will be imperative and of vital importance. These discussions will no longer happen at the tactical level where the focus is on doing things right to meet the commander's intent. The objective of these conversations will be to decide and agree on what is the right thing to do. For this purpose, they attend a one-year course. The objective of the course is to facilitate the officers' necessary shift from the tactical level of command to the operational and strategic level.

Identified Complexity of Required Communicative Skills

To reach any form of agreement, skillful interaction comes into play in the negotiation process. Such interaction includes:

- persuasion,
- perspective taking,
- suspension of judgement and personal expectations,
- belief revision,
- effective communication, and
- objection-handling.

A perfect command of the English language (i.e., grammar, vocabulary, morphology, and syntax) does not suffice to achieve this type of communicative interaction. The ability to speak a language easily, understandably, and quickly while feeling at ease in a conversation is not strong enough for this purpose. The officer also needs to master nuances, innuendo, the power of syntactic variation, and idiomatic language. Fluency needs to be coupled with accuracy. This is not a simple arithmetic addition. It is an equation in which it is necessary to add what lies beyond the grammar and vocabulary of the language – the ability to grasp the meaning of cultural, structural, behavioral, and sociolinguistic patterns: how they operate, how they are different from an officer's own culture, and how an officer must handle them. The equation demonstrates that officers need to reach a native-like second language competence in order to be fully interoperable with their English-speaking counterparts.

English Department Courses for High-Level Language Development

To help the officers reach this ambitious goal, the English Studies Department has designed three courses. The officers can choose one of these courses based on their individual objectives for the second part of their career.

Academic Writing and Public-Speaking Course

The Academic Writing and Public-Speaking course allows learners to write their research paper in English in collaboration with a British or American institution, usually a think-tank or a university. They work with a research advisor from the partner organisation and are mentored by a British or American writing coach. The coaches' role is to help learners structure and edit their paper in a way that will be appealing to the Anglophone readership across the Channel or across the Atlantic.

The aim of the course is to develop key leadership skills—such as critical analysis, persuasive argumentation, competent writing, and confident public speaking—to be fully interoperable in an Anglophone professional context. The process is designed to give the officers the confidence to interact effectively and comfortably with English-speaking counterparts in future staff work, using a student-led project of research, writing, and speaking that results in a paper (<6000 words) and oral presentation.

Networking, Public Speaking, and Events Course

The Networking, Public-Speaking, and Events course introduces learners to differing approaches to building a network. The coach focuses on the techniques that will sustain the officers' efforts to network within the Anglophone community, such as pitching, self-introduction, and quick-thinking.

The network the officers build by attending events weekly will support the organisation of an international symposium in collaboration with a British think tank. This is a student-led project during which they will regularly interact with British partners to choose the topic of the conference, the speakers, the moderators, the guests, and so on.

Beyond extending the officers' networks in the target countries, the course develops their ability to communicate effectively in English in a range of different contexts. As well, the course focuses on developing the officers' public speaking skills along with their ability to promote their work and ideas.

Debating, Research, and Public Speaking Course

The Debating, Research, and Public-Speaking course offers the students the opportunity to delve deeply into the fundamentally British and American tradition of debating. A debate coach will teach them the tenets of debate in the ways that they are taught in schools and universities in both countries. The officers learn how to construct a line of argument and build a case that will resonate, and hopefully, convince a British or American audience. They will learn the techniques that all debaters need to master, among which one would find:

- rebuttal,
- warrant-building,
- impact calculation,
- concession,
- extension,
- cross-examination, and
- many more techniques and skills.

The learning outcomes of this programme will support learners' leadership development by improving, in a second language, a number of aspects of good debate. These include, among others:

- critical thinking skills,
- delivery,

- strategic empathy,
- conflict resolution,
- quick-thinking, and
- research skills.

The coach will take them far beyond the theory of debating and argumentation by exposing them to *in situ* debates. Active participation in debate tournaments, strategy or policy competitions, and exhibition debates in an English-speaking environment thus serve to build understanding, experience, and skills.

Debate Programme Design

In 2012, the debate programme is the first of these courses that the English Studies Department set up. The department was founded in 2010, and the first courses in English were delivered in 2011. These were language courses and did not address the need the officers have to improve their cultural and professional interoperability with their English-speaking counterparts.

The Challenge of Developing Intercultural Competence As a Core Need

The stakeholders in the chain of command soon realised that the combination of cultural skills and professional knowledge was an essential requirement for the officers to be effective when working internationally at the operational and strategic level. They gave clear instructions to the department that can be summarised in a few words: "you need to teach them culture."

The challenge is that cultural awareness is an individual process and is acquired through individual experience. Culture is not a stable, unchanging concept used to label each inhabitant of a country. On the contrary, culture is a flowing and constantly evolving social force that will vary depending on each individual's life experience. Effective communication in a culturally different L2 environment is in fact "a complex, ongoing process that cannot be reduced to expedient labels and convenient dichotomies" (Kumaravadivelu, 2008).

To meet the challenge posed to the department, it was out of the question that there would be an opportunity to obtain substantial budget increase, pull the officers out of the college, and organise a several-month immersion in an English-speaking country. The decision came that the challenge could be met by designing an in-house programme that would help the officers acquire native-like competence in English.

The department was new in the making, and many difficulties lay in creating a course for educational standards never previously taught, particularly those with a focus on quality, distinctiveness, and performance. To draw an outline of this proposed course, brainstorming centered on the essential learning outcomes identified as a result of the needs analysis. Questions raised in the process included:

- What would lead the officers to master a perfect balance in the equation between accuracy, fluency, and cultural competence?

- What course would likely produce officers who would be fully interoperable with their English-speaking counterparts?
- What would sustain their efforts to reach and maintain a native-like language competence?

Gaining Perspective on the Challenge

Perspective taking was key in answering these questions. The department interviewed staff officers working in international headquarters to ask them what were the situations they felt were the most taxing. The most frequent answer by far was any situation where they had to set out a line of argument to defend a position. Most felt that however hard they tried, their arguments fell flat despite a very good command of the English language.

One cannot argue effectively in a second language without reaching native-like competence because an advanced level does not grant a student the understanding of what is an appealing line of argument in the target country and how to construct it to achieve significant convincing power. To better understand this drawback for the officers, the department analysed the differences in shaping arguments in France and in the UK or US.

In France, argumentation has been shaped by the rationalist school of philosophy which holds that the mind may apprehend some truths directly, without requiring the medium of the senses (Descartes, 2004/1637). That mindset is conditioned to prize principle above everything.

In contrast, British empiricism is the idea that the origin of all knowledge is sense experience. It emphasizes the role of experience and evidence in the formation of ideas, while discounting the notion of innate ideas (Bacon, 1620, in Sargett, 1999).

Pragmatism, a school of philosophy dominant in the United States in the first quarter of the twentieth century, is based on the principle that the practicality of ideas, policies, and proposals deserves merit (James, 1907). It stresses the priority of action over doctrine, of experience over fixed principles, and holds that ideas draw their truths from their verification (Rosenthal & Thayer, 2023). Empiricism and pragmatism are usually contrasted with rationalism.

The officers were translating into English conceptual lines of argument most likely without explaining the practicality of their principled extension. It is with this realisation that emerged the idea of setting up a debate programme for the officers. Putting them through a programme similar to the ones that exist in British or American schools, universities and military academies would most likely help them improve fluency, accuracy, and the understanding of their counterparts' mind-set, therefore reaching a native-like competence and becoming fully interoperable in an English-speaking environment.

Structure of the Programme

The programme is structured into two parts. The first semester focuses on a British approach to debating with workshops delivered by a London-based debate society, exhibition debates, tournaments with British institutions either in Paris or in London, and a study tour to London. The second semester is dedicated to American Parliamentary Debate and American Policy Debate with similar activities organised with American organisations and two study tours to the USA. The officers have three hours of class and a practice debate session on site every week throughout the year to learn about debate and to prepare for all the activities mentioned above.

Over the years, the debate coaches have always been British or American. Rather than being a disadvantage, this is a key asset to the programme as it offers the officers an opportunity to test their approaches on a mindset shaped by an academic journey in one of the target countries. It is very difficult to find a debate coach in Paris to deliver this programme as there are no debate programmes in schools or universities in France as there are in the US or the UK. The consequence is that the War College has to cap the number of students who can join the programme to preserve its effectiveness and offer individualised coaching for each participant.

The cohort receives a detailed presentation about the programme. They are provided a thorough explanation that it is not an English language class.

Selection Process

To select those who will join the programme amongst all the volunteers, individual interviews are carried out by the head of department, the debate coach, and alumni students from previous years. The officers need to prepare a three-minute opposition speech—or a first negative constructive speech in the American lingo—for the interview. Despite these officers never having done debating before, their attempts to demonstrate a different approach to argumentation, however clumsy they may be, gives some clear indication of the interviewee's understanding of the programme. Interviewees must also reflect on the reason why they want to join the programme as this will be the main topic of the follow-up conversation after the feedback to their short speech. The goal is to check that they come to the programme with the necessary open-mindedness to work on a different construct of argumentation. The importance of putting their focus on the learning process as opposed to only focusing on winning debates is discussed. It is crucial to manage their expectations.

Course Content and Tasks

Once the selection has been completed, the coach connects with his groups and starts the first class. This article will not go into the details of how the programme unfolds but will rather look at some salient points that have indicated that it undeniably buttresses the officers in the process of reaching native-like competence.

One of the first tasks for the debate coach is to ensure that learners embrace the fact that they will constantly be building lines of argumentation that are structurally very different from what forms their comfort zone. This doesn't mean that their approach is no longer valid. Rather, it means accepting that there are circumstances where their approach is not successful enough and that it is necessary to learn and master a different way of arguing in those specific circumstances.

The first step is to understand what an evidence-based approach entails. Once a claim is clearly outlined, the use of objective evidence will inform how the argument is designed. In-depth research is necessary to collect relevant evidence. The officers are highly encouraged to do extensive reading for that purpose. This will not only serve the preparation for any debate, it will also support the journey to native-like proficiency because reading significantly improves vocabulary-building, structure, and syntax (see Bernhardt, this issue). It is also a strong vehicle to acquire sociocultural knowledge (Uemura, 2020). All students who have reached such a level have in common that they are insatiable readers (Leaver & Atwell, 2002).

On any given motion to debate, the officers are required to bring into class the material they have selected from their readings. Each one of them is asked to brief the rest of the group on how the evidence they have found effectively supports or opposes the motion. The coach facilitates the conversation and helps narrow down the list to the pieces of evidence that generate consensus. Their expertise is invaluable, especially on motions that deal with defence issues or geopolitics. They will know how to cherry-pick the most relevant evidence. To do so, they will explore areas they want to learn more about and this is the bedrock of motivation. Their analytical skills are put to the test. Not only is this invaluable for their professional future, it is a thrilling part of the learning process. As they are all from different services and all have different professional experiences, they will be bringing in completely different perspectives on how to solve the problem, i.e. how to best demonstrate the proposition or opposition side of the debate. They will confront their perspective in class and do the work of questioning their assumptions in the light of a variety of approaches to the same question. This is an important stepping stone to broaden their mind enough to reach a native-like level. It is also a central part in the process of transformative learning which is the chosen approach in Ecole de Guerre (Cleret, 2021; Collin, 2021).

Encouraging extensive individual reading, asking the students to bring in their own material, and giving them the opportunity to brief in class caters to varying types of learners. Ectenic, or "fractional," learners and synoptic, or "comprehensive," learners can organise their reading and research work in the framework that best suits their learning style. They can adjust the right kind and quantity of work that serves them best. Individualisation is at the core of transformative pedagogy, and it is foundational to the development of native-like proficiency as there are as many ways to reach this level as there are learners.

Debate pushes the students to question and argue against preconceived notions through the formulation of the question "why." The first step in debate is to question notions that seem self-evident and understand the source of those preconceived notions. A valid argument relies on a warrant, which is an explanation of why the claim is true (Nordquist, 2020). Warrant-building may also be referred to as the chain of reasoning. However, there is not a right way to build a chain of reasoning. The method will differ for each individual. When developing a chain of reasoning in favour of a specific position, debaters are not asked to write a simplistic list of arguments in favour or against the topic.

On the contrary, they are encouraged to start by asking questions such as why are we having this debate? Why do the key actors act the way they do? What are the perspectives and priorities that shape their attitudes?

The officers usually handle value-based and norms-based debates. Values are abstract concepts generally understood as priorities that will serve the greater good. Norms generally refer to what is standard and permissible action in society; they play a major role in maintaining social order and stability. It is most likely impossible to win a debate without delivering some thorough perspective taking and belief revision in order to fully grasp what are the opponents' values that defines the norms they operate under. This can be achieved by suspending any prescriptive assumptions on a different cultural approach in order to understand it. With every debate, their social and cultural knowledge of the target country vastly expands and strengthens their foundation to build native-like competence.

Once all the reading has been done, the discussion on the relevant evidence, the right questions asked, the coach can lead the officers into the pre-writing phase of the first proposition speech or first constructive affirmative speech. They will brainstorm the best strategy for the warrant, which is an explanation of why the claim is true. In other words, warrant-building is the chain of reasoning. They will discuss the wording and the associated lexical fields. The coach will use this opportunity to do vocabulary-building and ask the officers to use the new words and colocations in the first draft of the speech. The second draft of the speech will improve syntax, consistency and structure. A final review will focus on the impact of the wording and effective flow between the claim and the evidence may it be in sentences, paragraphs or the speech as a whole. This ensures the intended impact on the intended audience.

Practice debates will put the chain of reasoning to the test. Due to the stress induced by the activity, the officers will highly rely on their procedural memory to deliver their speech and manage the questions. Thus, it is in these moments that fossilisation is revealed. For years, the students simply ignore this phenomenon as it never really caused an issue in the conversation with native speakers. It is a very different story in a structured and regimented debate. While fossilised errors will highly hinder the speaker's delivery and impact, it will also impede the necessary engagement with the opposite team because these mistakes will prevent them from understanding the chain of reasoning. As these mistakes will literally disrupt the flow of the chain of reasoning and prevent the speaker from reaching his/her desired end-state, he/she will become immediately aware of the dead weight this is for him/her and the urgency to deal with the problem. The coach will sit down with the student, analyse the error, and help him/her break down the reason why they occur. They will together set new goals out of the comfort zone that is fostering fossilisation. These goals can be achieved through regular exercises or drills. They will then take the discussion to the rest of the group so that peer correction can take place every time the inaccurate language is used. The same awareness develops regarding compensation strategies. The officers realised that to win a case, one cannot be content in coming quite close to what they mean or to be satisfied with the idea that the interlocutor has roughly understood the main idea in the argument. They are ready to step out of the comfortable area of compensation strategies to make the necessary efforts to reach lexical precision and structural accuracy.

Debate Tours and Learning Expeditions

After the classes on the theory of debate and the preparation phase comes the *in situ* debates that occur in Paris, London, or the USA. Study tours are carefully designed to give the officers the opportunity to be in situations in which they can thrive only if they use native-like resources. This is achieved by enrolling them in debate tournaments or in strategy competitions. A debate tournament on the American circuit has no space to cater to the specific needs of L2 speakers. The officers will have to compete at the same level as the native speakers. A strategy competition organised by the US Army War College does not leave a chance to contenders who would need more time to pull their case together.

Knowledge of State Apparatus

The department devises study tours that appropriately meet the officers' needs. In addition to the *in situ* debate opportunities, these trips are also learning expeditions that offer visits, meetings and briefings in the military and government institutions in London or Washington DC. They deepen their knowledge and understanding of the state apparatus and the military decision-making process thus increasing their level of interoperability with their counterparts.

Collaborative Workshops

The trips give the officers access to workshops that do not exist in France and are not deliverable on-line. They work with leading figures of the debate community who deliver mini-seminars for them during which collaborative exercises and activities in pair are central. The quality of this type of in-person training is difficult to replicate on-line, and the workshop leaders are rarely available to travel to France.

Improvement of Delivery

In another vein, they also work with artists to hone their delivery, their command of stress patterns, and pronunciation. French is a syllable-timed language, so equal emphasis is given to each syllable. This is quite unlike English, which is a stress-timed language. French learners struggle with this all their lives, and, once they have reached an advanced level, these issues are deeply fossilised. It is common knowledge that it is recommended to teach through music at higher levels because the students can actually hear, identify the modulations of voice, and easily reproduce them. Teaching through music is usually very unfamiliar to them, and it creates the necessary disruption to push them out of the fossilisation comfort zone. For this purpose, they engage with hip-hop artists who design a freestyle rap workshop for them. Not only does this improve their pronunciation, articulation, and delivery, but it also sharpens their improvisation skills.

Improvisation Skills

Mastered improvisation is key to leaders. Otherwise, how would they deal with disruption and crises? In order to thrive in times of uncertainty, it is an imperative to be able to think on one's feet and act fast—without an instruction manual. Improvisation may seem incompatible with the well-defined processes that govern command and control, but it is in fact key to organizational agility as capable improvisers will steer their teams through crises and paradigm shifts. In order to deliver this in an English-speaking environment, the French advanced learners will have to reach native-like competence. For that purpose, they are trained to perform impromptu debates. These happen without any preparation but with some advanced and prepossessed knowledge of the topic. This allows the officers to point at the relevant issues related to the topic, include some personal examples, be direct, and speak with conviction.

After thorough practice, officers can test these skills in impromptu debate tournaments or extemporaneous speech contexts with native speakers. They are supported to perform the best they can. Nonetheless, this is not the most important goal of these engagements. Officers are highly encouraged to observe and to listen to how the other speakers perform.

Observation of Native Speakers

The officers are well aware of the difference between a native speaker and a proficient non-native speaker. They therefore know that they can draw from this observation a list of words, colocations, or phrases that they found particularly useful to signpost the line of argumentation or the cross-examination. For example, some picked up the expression "moving on" to signal the transition from one argument to another. In cross examination, they noted a useful response to hint at the opponent's biased line of questioning: "that's a loaded question." They then incorporate these into their own speeches and communication. A dictionary will never equate the meticulous observation of native speakers.

More Elaborate Speaking Patterns

Advanced students are capable of delivering a speech and taking part in a conversation. To reach native-like competence, the learners must be willing to engage in and learn how to master far more elaborate forms of communication, especially those which will make or break their discussion in a professional environment.

Debating offers an opportunity for all learners to gain control over some of these communication patterns. For example, rebuttal is a very useful technique to respond to opposing arguments. The speaker will recapitulate the argument while clearly signposting its structure. The speaker will then explain why it is incorrect and/or why it is flawed. The speaker will finish by linking back to his/her arguments and show how to respond to the flaws.

Another example is how debaters learn to manage requests for points of information that are very disruptive to the flow of their speech. This will translate into skillful objection-handling when in meetings with their English-speaking counterparts.

Debate Flowing

In order to be very accurate in any response to an argument, the officers are taught how to flow a debate. Flowing is a specific technique to take notes and keep track of what is happening in the debate. This is absolutely crucial to make sure that the most important arguments are answered and precisely follow what the opposite team is coming up with. Debaters need to flow downwards so as to create a vertical column for each speech. They identify each type of argument—topicality, disadvantages, benefits, and counterplans. They write down every piece of evidence with its source. They then write down answers to arguments right next to the argument that is being answered. By the end of the debate, they have the whole structure of the debate in front of them. Before the rebuttal, they can circle or highlight the arguments that absolutely need to be addressed. This skill is transferable to any professional situation as it will be an effective lever for developing fluent, accurate, and meaningful points in any negotiation.

Assessments

The programme focuses on formative assessment rather than summative assessment. In-process evaluation allows focusing on the learning curve rather than educational outcomes measured by a test and a score.

Feedback

Each practice debate or *in situ* activity acts as a check and balance of the learners' progress and the effectiveness of their own practice. Each offers the opportunity for individual, in-process feedback. The coach and the officer will discuss what was achieved in the debate, what wasn't, and why there were some shortfalls. If a mental block is identified, the coach can adapt the instructional approach, the teaching material, or the content to better fit the student's needs. The student has now labelled some potential issues and can take action to solve them. The student can determine his own goals to increase his achievements. The personalisation of the learning experience maintains a high level of motivation and creates a group of self-regulated learners.

Reflection

After each *in situ* experience, the officers are encouraged to pause and reflect about what it means to them and what they learnt from it. The programme strongly recommends journaling and, beyond that, the building of learners' own dictionary. This new, unique, individual wordbook would not only be a list of the new words or colocations picked up but also what some concepts mean to the learners. They might have found out how they specifically want to apply some of the leadership skills they developed. They might better understand what their public-speaking style is. They might better sense what type of leadership is relevant to them.

Self-reflection is key to reaching a native-like competence as this means more than mastering the language. It also involves cultural competence, behavioural change, and intellectual agility. This is the reason why transformative pedagogy seems to be a relevant approach for this programme. Learning in transformative theory involves a change in each individual's meaning structures through the practice of critical self-examination. This means accepting that past assumptions need to be assessed, reviewed critically and their validity checked. As written above, before, during and after debates, they reflect on answering the "why" questions. This thinking process results in a better understanding of themselves and the biases aligned with their judgement in decision-making. Debating is about experimenting what a policy or plan would look like even if it seems unrealistic in the eyes of the speaker. The discussion is not oriented around whether the plan will occur or not but rather on whether it should occur or not. The added value for the military is the practice of decision-making skills through creativity, self-examination, and adaptation in the process of reaching a native-like competence.

Looking toward the Future

Recently, the department has tried to push the experience further by arguing for all activities to happen in blended teams. Each team in the debate is composed of French officers and British or American counterparts.

Teaming makes the activity far less adversarial and brings the officers' focus back on the content, the learning process, the emergence of new ideas and the actual engagement. The objective is to make the learning experience about dialogue and defence engagement in order to offer learners the most favourable environment to reach full interoperability with their counterparts.

Teaming takes advantage of the positive elements brought to the learning experience by the debate programme. Beyond that, the blending creates a natural segue from self-reflection to team-member reflection that necessarily must negotiate the social divide and create the personal transformation needed to engender the cultural, cross-cultural, and intercultural understanding that is critical to the development of native-like proficiency.

References

Cleret, E. (2021). The challenges of implementing transformative pedagogy. In B. L. Leaver, D. E. Davidson, & C. Campbell, eds. *Transformative language learning and teaching* (pp. 61-68). Cambridge, UK: Cambridge University Press.

Collin, J. (2021). Immersion and transformative pedagogy in the French Language Department of the French War College. In B. L. Leaver, D. E. Davidson, & C. Campbell, eds. *Transformative language learning and teaching* (pp. 129-136). Cambridge, UK: Cambridge University Press.

Descartes, R. (2004/1637). *A discourse on method: Meditations and principles.* Translated by J. Veitch. London: Orion Publishing Group.

Ehrman, M. E., & Leaver, B. L. (2003). Cognitive styles in the service of language learning. *System 31*(3): 395-415.

James, W. (1907). *Pragmatism, a new name for some old ways of thinking: Popular lectures on philosophy.* New York: Longmans, Green, and Company.

Kumaravadivelu, B. (2008) *Cultural globalization in language education.* New Haven, CT: Yale University Press.

Leaver, B. L., & Atwell, S. (2002). Preliminary qualitative findings of a study of the processes leading to the Advanced Professional Proficiency level (ILR 4). In B. L. Leaver & B. S. Shekhtman, eds. *Developing professional-level foreign language proficiency* (pp. 260-279). Cambridge, UK: Cambridge University Press.

Moslemi, N., & Dastgoshadeh, A. (2017). The relationship between cognitive styles and young adult learners' preferences for written corrective feedback. *HOW Journal* 24(2): 11-34.

Nordquist, R. (August 26, 2020). Warrants in the Toulmin Model of Argument. Downloaded from thoughtco.com/warrant-argument-1692602.

Rosenthal, S. B. and Thayer, . H.S. (2023, July 11). *pragmatism. Encyclopedia Britannica.* https://www.britannica.com/topic/pragmatism-philosophy.

Sargett, R-M. (1999). *Francis Bacon: Selected philosophical works.* Cambridge, UK: Hackett Publishing Group.

Uemura, A. (2020). Potential of extensive reading as a means of intercultural education: A pilot study. *Extensive Reading World Congress Proceedings* 5: 41-49.

About the Author

Emilie Alice Cleret is a Franco-British academic and educator, who specializes in transformative pedagogy for leaders. Currently the Head of the English Studies Department for French Higher Military Education, she has created and manages academic programs for both the Ecole de Guerre (the French War College) and the Centre des hautes études militaires. She has dedicated her 21-year-career to designing and launching English-language programs for military leadership and managing their teaching and administrative teams, forging links between France, the US, and the UK, and leading seminars on debating, public speaking, networking, and transformative learning. After two years of study at the Maison d'Education de la Légion d'Honneur, she completed her Bachelor's and Master's degrees at La Sorbonne and teaching certification from the French Ministry of National Education. She taught English as a second language in the French public education system for six years and served as teacher and course designer at the Army NCO Basic Training Academy in France. She has been the French representative to the NATO Bureau of International Language Coordination since 2017 and manages partnerships between France and the US, including with RUSI, State Department-Global Engagement Center, National Defense University, Institute for State Effectiveness, and George Washington University. She is the recipient of the prestigious Chevalier de l'Ordre des Palmes Académiques and the author of articles and book chapters on transformative learning.

Helping Learners Achieve the Distinguished Level of Proficiency

James E. Bernhardt, Foreign Service Institute (USA)

Abstract

This article proposes that a task all learners who have attained superior levels of proficiency and who wish to achieve the distinguished level have in common is the need to double the size of their vocabulary. The article suggests that instructional designs for distinguished level training should include massive amounts of input: reading, listening, and watching. It also proposes a number of ways, all vocabulary based, to evaluate whether materials are at-level for learners and advocates for materials that are appropriate to the individual learners' needs, objectives and interests.

The article takes a close look at the goals of higher-level programs and notes that not all learners working towards distinguished levels of proficiency have the same end goals in mind. Their objectives, at this level, differ from learner to learner. Their objectives and the needs of the organizations that fund their training also surely differ from the characteristics of distinguished level proficiency implied by the ACTFL standards and the ILR skill level descriptions: eloquence, membership in the cloistered elect of the well-educated, and the ability to speak in ways that approximate written texts.

The article asserts that students have a set of rights, which, when exercised, may change the trajectory of each course even midstream. It examines paths towards success, rejecting the use of Bloom's taxonomy and suggesting the use of design thinking approaches to creating an instructional program. Attention is paid to techniques for evaluating the appropriateness of materials for training, with a special focus on words, word families, and the importance of knowing the size of a learner's word bank and speed at which the student reads. When instructors know their learners well, they can, working with the learners and stakeholders, create a learning plan for each learner which meets their precise needs.

Keywords: vocabulary, objectives, rights, Bloom's taxonomy, text profiling

Εν ἀρχή ἦν ὁ λόγος (In the beginning was the Word.)

"It dawns on him that this is the language of all these people around him, this mix of people who are always on the road, instead of some language carefully assembled in a single place for the benefit of a few" Tokarczuk (2022, p. 754).

Language learning for students approaching distinguished level of proficiency is challenging, interesting, and teacher-assisted. This restatement reflects nearly 40 years of programming beyond ILR 3 at the Foreign Service Institute and in a few other programs elsewhere, such as the Defense Language Institute Foreign Language Center and NASA. The teacher-assisted requirement, which can appear contrary to assumptions, has been confirmed by qualitative and quantitative research (Leaver & Atwell, 2002; Franke, 2020).

The program of study for students at this level should be balanced among the four strands:

- meaning-focused input;
- meaning-focused output;
- study of forms and structures; and
- work on fluency (speed and ease).

For teachers working at this level, teaching is more about planning and giving feedback than about lecturing and explaining. Planning, by far the most important thing a teacher does, ensures that materials and activities are both relevant to the students and at their levels. Level is largely determined by vocabulary, and, especially, the frequency of words and grammatical forms.

A well balanced-language study program, a concept developed by Paul Nation (2013, 2017), is essential for all stages of language learning and especially important for those moving to the Distinguished level. Nation's design for language learning and teaching, called the Four Strands, is research based. It is not a new methodology or set of teaching activities. It encourages teachers to continue doing what has worked well for them while encouraging them to think about and adjust their work to achieve balance. While all four stands, input, output, structure and fluency, get equal attention, Nation presents them in order of importance. Meaning focused input (reading and listening) comes first.

In this article, we focus primarily on the meaning-focused input strand of a well-balanced program.

Focus on Meaning

For most instructors working in traditional language programs, a focus on form (or forms) (Doughty & Williams, 1998) comes most naturally and most easily, and tends to take up most of the instructional time and energy. And while the instructors' explanations of the things they call grammar play a key role in helping students move toward higher levels of proficiency, they are not the most important aspect of a good program. The focus-on-form strand is key to a good language acquisition program since it includes a good amount vocabulary acquisition, the deliberate learning of words, which does play a key role in the student journey to proficiency. The size of a student's word bank is a key, if not *the* key, measure of her/his proficiency.

Meaning-focused input (reading and listening/watching) should be in the driver's seat, especially for students working toward the highest levels of proficiency. Through massive amounts of reading, listening, and watching videos on YouTube and like platforms, students experience words and structures in multiple contexts, at multiple registers, and with multiple neighbors. Through the experience of reading massive amounts of texts and watching and listening to videos and movies, students begin to internalize the likelihood or improbability of collocations, various meanings of words, and their registers and histories of their use. Students begin to make the transition from speaking in their own way to speaking in the ways of their new language.

Meaning-focused output ought to take up about a quarter of the students' learning time. Students at the Foreign Service Institute love to talk. One of the keys to a good output-training session, however, is to be sure that the students and instructor are focused on meaning, not on form. At lower levels of proficiency, a good meaning-focused assignment would be to ask the students to "talk about what they did over the weekend." An assignment that is not meaning-focused would be to ask the students to talk about their weekends using a specific list of five verbs in the past tense. That would be a form-focused assignment.

Fluency

The fluency strand takes up the remaining quarter of a well-balanced program. An easy and traditional way to formulate the goals of this strand is to say that students ought to be doing what they already know how to do but to do it faster and with greater ease.

Building fluency, increasing speed, especially in reading, is an essential component of the FSI program. Students need to be able to read at rates approaching 250 words a minute, the average reading speed of a typical native speaker of Russian (IRIS, 2023). Experience has indicated that many teachers do not know their students' reading speeds, but they should. If students are reading fewer than 100 words a minute, typical of FSI students, they are not coming close to having an authentic reading experience. At rates that slow, it is hard for students to remember what was happening at the beginning of the sentence when they get to the end. While not as part of this article, there are many suggestions online for how teachers can help their students increase reading speed.

Vocabulary

For learners moving from the Superior Level to the Distinguished Level, from the ILR 3 to the ILR 4, the biggest task by far is the acquisition of vocabulary. Learners successfully achieving the Superior Level, or the ILR 3, have mastered most of the grammatical patterns and most, but not all, of the structures of the language.

One of the major improvements in the new Interagency Language Roundtable's (ILR) skill level descriptions at the S/4 level is its specific reference to vocabulary frequency: "Vocabulary is consistently extensive and includes low frequency items" (ILR, 2022). Low frequency is a term of art meaning word families in the 9000-word band or higher. The first three bands of the most frequent words are considered high frequency words. The highest frequency word in English is *the*, which makes up around 6% of most English language texts. Mid-frequency words (word families) are those that appear in the fourth to the ninth thousand bands, and low frequency words that appear in bands above nine.

The Russian Test for Foreigners (TORFL, 2023) focuses on vocabulary size, and, in the experience of this author, the Russians have come closest to getting it right. The Russians say that students at the highest levels of proficiency should know 20,000 units, with 8,000 of them being active. The Russians do not tell us what they mean by units, but their numbers seem to be in the right ballpark.

Nation and Waring (2020) claim that in order to have an authentic reading experience with unsimplified texts, which ought to be the goal of every distinguished-level program, the reader should command a vocabulary of some 9000-word families. Hacking and Tschirner (2017) found that readers at the ILR skill level 3 command some 5000-word families.

The task for students hoping to move from the ILR 3, ACTFL Superior level is daunting but clear. Learners moving from the Superior Level to the Distinguished level need to double the size of their vocabularies.

What does a learner need to do in order to achieve proficiency at the Distinguished range? In order to move from the ILR 3 to the ILR 4, moving to the Distinguished Level, the learner needs to acquire over 4000 new word families. Most of these new words will be in the mid-frequency range (3000 to 9000) and some from the low frequency range (over 9000-word families). In order to do that, the learner needs to read massive amounts of text and do substantial amounts of deliberate learning of vocabulary. The learner will need help from a good instructor in picking texts and understanding words in context. The reader will need lots and lots of time to read. This is all done in the meaning-focused portion of the FSI Beyond Three program.

Program Design

What does the instructor need to do in order to facilitate the learner's move to the Distinguished level? The instructor gathers enough information about the learner's abilities and the learner's goals in order to plan an effective course of study. The instructor gathers information about the learners' developing vocabulary bank through formative assessments, which supply the student and instructor with precisely the right information to support the kind of feedback that will enhance learning.

The instructor needs to know the size of the learner's vocabulary bank and be able to track it as it grows. The instructor also needs to have a clear picture of the size of the language, in terms of vocabulary, that the student will need once at the Distinguished level. The instructor, along with the student, needs a fairly accurate picture of the learner's reading speed (which, by the end of the program, should be approaching 250 words per minute). Finally, the instructor needs to know what kinds of texts the student will find interesting and relevant. With that information in hand, the instructor is ready to plan an outstanding program of study individualized to the needs of the learner.

Meaning-focused Reading

Meaning-focused input is, for the instructor, both the easiest and hardest part of the program. Meaning focused input requires planning and preparation on the part of the teacher. The instructor's job in delivering an outstanding meaning-focused input strand is to know the student's strengths and weaknesses, vocabulary size, command of structure and discourse, ability to pronounce words accurately, and level of critical thinking skills. The instructor also needs to know the materials available and how and when those materials will best support the learners. The instructor should know which materials are at the learner's level, which ones are relevant to the learner's future needs, and which ones might be interesting to the learner.[1]

One way to judge the probability that a learner can have an authentic reading experience with a text is to look at the vocabulary in the text in terms of word frequency. It is safe to assume that learners acquire words in some sort of frequency order. Since spaced repetition is key to learning, seeing words frequently means that they have a good chance of learning those words and learning them more quickly than ones they see infrequently.

It is important to note that learners tend to learn words in frequency order. Why does this happen? Because learners see high frequency words (the most frequent 3000 words) more frequently than they do mid-frequency words (words in the 4000-to-9000-word bands). This does not happen in lockstep. One doesn't learn the first word before the second or the fifty-first before the fifty-second. But generally, learners acquire the first thousand words before they learn the second or third thousand. Yet, as they have contact with texts, they will pick up words in the fourth and fifth, or even the fifteenth thousand-word frequency band while still working on the first or second thousand-word families. While it may be possible to learn words from reading and listening only, the use of deliberate vocabulary learning techniques can speed the process greatly.

An anecdote from my own (and not unique) experience learning Russian many years ago at a Midwest university may help to explicate the situation. The Russian teacher of our third-year class assigned the ten words in Russian ending in -мя that are neuter (имя, время, etc.) After passing the -мя test, I next saw the word вымя (udder) in a text 48 years later. I believe that I remembered that word from the first time that I saw it since I was stunned by the fact that Russian had such a common word (I grew up on a farm) when I had always thought of Russian as the language of beautiful poetry and profound philosophy. I signed up for Russian in order to read Tolstoy and Dostoevsky. I have yet to meet another of the ten words, темя (sinciput), in the wild. While I still believe all of my Russian teachers were patient and wonderful, I have come to wonder whether an assignment that set me up for a reading task 48 years in the future was a good one.

---

1. See related discussion (Leaver, this volume) of the zone of proximal development being used together with formative assessment to help learners move from Superior to Distinguished levels of proficiency,

Arranging Authentic Reading Experiences

In order for an instructor to judge the readability of a text for a specific student, the instructor needs to know the size of student's vocabulary and the nature of the words in the text. So, how does an instructor estimate the size of a learner's vocabulary? Or know which texts are going to be at the appropriate level for individual learners?

Hu and Nation (2000) suggest that in order to have an authentic reading experience, the reader needs to know 95% to 98% of the words in the text. At 95%, the students may need help from their instructors. Below 90%, the students are no longer having an authentic reading experience.

The concept of "at level" begins, in many ways, with Stephen Krashen's (1997) concept of comprehensible input. Krashen argues that an approach based on comprehensible input is valid and appropriate for language programs and can solve some of the problems that learners face. The challenge, of course, is to figure out a way to judge the probability that one text or another will be comprehensible to a particular student.

In a review of Krashen's work, Lichtman and VanPatten (2021) write that Krashen claimed that students could understand input that was at the i+1 level, i.e., the level that is just beyond the students' current level, but would not be able to understand input that was at *i*+5, i.e., input that was well above the students' level. They note, though, that neither *i* nor +1 were defended terms. Yet, Lichtman and VanPatten stress the essentiality of comprehensible input for language acquisition. Experience at the FSI shows that there is reason to make this claim.[2]

Determining Students' Reading Levels

A key question in designing language programs is how can the instructors and their students know what their levels are. Were it possible to know how many and which words students knew, it would be possible to judge the probability that a student could have an authentic reading experience with the text.

Knowing what words the learners know and what words are in the text they would like to read, we could judge whether a text is readable for a particular student. In other words, with two key pieces of information it would be possible to guess that a particular text might be at level. At least a couple of ways to assess students' level do exist.

A visit to the children's section of the local library may reveal one possible approach to the problem. Bookmarks designed to help young readers judge the readability of a text for themselves can serve as aids for language learners as well. Bookmarks provided by childrenslibrarylady.com suggest using the Five Finger Rule:

1. choose a book you are interested in reading;
2. read a full page in the middle of the book;

---

2. At the same time, one does not need *experience* to know that the *logic* holds: incomprehensible input would be a memory overload, trying to store and recall what would essentially sound or look like nonsense. Memory needs some kind of key, or coding, to store information (McLeod, 2023).

3. hold up a finger for each word you do not know;
4. when you get to the end of the page, count the number of fingers you have up.

One finger, the book is too easy, try another book. Two fingers the book is just right. Three fingers, the book will be a little challenging, but could be fun. Four fingers, the book will be difficult to read; you may need some help. And five fingers, this book is too hard for now. This is a neat, easy way to apply a sort of probability formula for the readability of a book. It is easy to see how the Five Finger Rule approximates more complex and expensive approaches to judging the appropriateness of specific texts for specific students. And, further, it moves judgements about the appropriateness of the level of the text from the course designer to the student while still retaining an individualized, yet research-based, foundation for making curricular decisions.

In *Measuring Second Language Vocabulary Acquisition*, James Milton (2009) suggests a fairly simple and reliable methodology for estimating learners' vocabulary size. Students look at lists of words selected from various frequency bands and tick the ones they believe they know. Words representing each frequency band include a small number of made-up words included to make it possible to adjust the scores for guessing. The answer shows approximately where the student is in terms of word frequency bands. With that information, the instructor can begin selecting texts that are likely to be at level. Milton gives sample vocabulary range tests at the end of his book and clear directions for producing and scoring tests.

Some instructors have argued that just ticking boxes does not give a clear picture of students' knowledge of words. They have argued for translation tests, collocation tests, multiple-choice tests and other formats, which they believe will give a clearer picture. They may be right. However, the amount of work involved in producing other kinds of tests makes them too difficult and expensive for most instructors and institutions to use on a routine and ongoing basis.

Here is another fairly reliable way to do a dead reckoning of learners' vocabulary. Learn from the students, or from their records, how many contact hours of instruction they have had studying the language and multiply that number by 4.5. If, for instance, a student has completed four semesters of intensive study at 75 contact hours per semester, the student has had 300 contact hours and will likely know somewhere in the vicinity of 1350 words. A student who has completed a basic course of study for a category 3 language[3] at the Foreign Service Institute will have had a little fewer than 1100 hours of instruction and will likely know somewhere in the vicinity of 5000 words, give or take. This means that, if Hacking and Tschirner (2017) are correct and an ILR 3, the training goal for the FSI program, comes in at some 5000 words, students will be at the entry point to attempt to achieve the Distinguished level.

---

3. State Department divides languages into four categories, based on difficulty of learning for a native speaker of English, as determined by research on thousands of students over three decades. Category 3 languages include Russian, other Slavic languages, and a few others that differ distinctly from English linguistically and culturally.

Can a student acquire more than 4.5 words per instructional hour? Yes, of course; if the instructional design focuses on vocabulary acquisition and includes components of dedicated study of vocabulary, student acquisition numbers can be pushed up.

Does it matter if the numbers derived using the shortcut are off? Not really. Since vocabulary size is looked at in thousand-word bands if the number is off by 500 (say the student knows 1850 words rather than the expected 1350), the student would still be working in the second thousand-word band, meaning the student still has a way to go before having acquired a significant quantity of the high frequency words in the language.

Instructors working with less-commonly-taught languages or almost-never-taught languages may be able to assume that their students know most of the words they have taught them, keep a list of those words, and use that list to make judgments about whether learners might be able to read a certain text. Instructors working with languages widely studied will have to pick a strategy for measuring vocabulary size since students will have a range of language learning experiences and may not all know the same set of words. It is also worth noting that students who spend a considerable amount of time on the Internet reading and watching, many know words not covered in their formal programs of study.

Once the approximate size of a learner's word bank has been determined, the task of selecting texts at the appropriate level can take place.

Text Selection

As we turn to consider texts, we should consider Zipf's law (see earlier reference). Put very simply, Zipf tells us that we see high frequency words more often than we see low frequency words. Zipf tells us that the most common word in English is *the*, and that, knowing it, we know 6% of most texts. If we add the second most common word, we pick up another 3% and now recognize some 9% of the texts we are reading. The next word will give us 2% (6 decided by rank yields frequency, again over simplifying), etc., etc. It is clear that the more high-frequency words a student knows, the more he/she will recognize in any text. In many languages, the top 100 most frequent words in the language give nearly 50% coverage!

One must consider, though, how many of these high-frequency words are function words that carry almost no meaning and how many others are words that have many meanings.

Learning the high-frequency words provides coverage. Learning wisely chosen mid- and low-frequency words provides meaning. Knowing the learners' subject area, teachers can help guide the learner toward those words that will supply the most meaning and avoid the thousands of words students will not likely see. (If they do see them, they can, of course, look them up.) This is an important concept when designing instruction for the superior or lower levels.

In order to achieve the Distinguished level of proficiency, learners have to have learned nearly all of the high- and mid-frequency level words, and wisely chosen low-frequency words. Learners achieving the Distinguished level need 9000-word families, minimum.

So, how to evaluate or profile texts in order to know that there is a high probability that the learner can have an authentic reading experience with the text? When working with a student beginning the journey from Superior to Distinguished levels of proficiency, it is fair to assume a foundation of 5000-words families and move up. What percentage of coverage do the most frequent 9000-word families yield for a given text? If the student is midway through the program, what percentage of coverage would the top 7000-word families give, or top 8000-word families give? If the number is 95% or higher, the text is ideal for the learner. If it is lower, the learner is not ready for it yet.

By using Lawrence Anthony's AntWord Profiler, a software program that is available free online,[4] it is possible to see how the words in a text distribute over thousand-word frequency bands. Working with frequency lists, the AntWord Profiler produces a table telling the instructor the percentages of coverage for each thousand-word band. The instructor can then make judgments about which stage in the learner's journey texts become appropriate.

Using the AntWord profiler and well-made word lists composed by instructors or, better yet, by students, any text in text format can be checked for readability. The biggest task for instructional designers for this approach to assessing readability is making or acquiring reliable word family frequency lists.

By using Lawrence Anthony's AntWord Profiler or any equivalent software (currently, none has yet appeared to have been developed), it is possible to assess any text and judge whether students can read a text fluently, whether it is going to be appropriately challenging, whether they will need significant guidance from their teacher, or whether the text is too difficult for them. In order to do this, only three things are needed: 1) a desired-for-reading text in electronic format; 2) a word family frequency list relevant to students' needs; and 3) a little experience with the software. Once these items have been assembled, the following can happen:

1. An instructor takes any text that is out of copyright (1925 publication date or earlier when this article is being written) and replace low frequency words with more frequently used ones.
2. A judgment can be made whether current news articles, following fair use rules, are appropriate for students.
3. Several documents can be examined, such as units in instructional materials, in order to see whether the type of spaced repetition learners need is being achieved.

Finding good word frequency lists is easiest for English and teachers and students of English as a second or foreign language. Word frequency lists exist for English. Once downloaded, the AntWord Profiler automatically provides lists of the top 2000-word families (alphabetized) and a list of some 750 academic words.

Many word frequency lists are available on the Internet for a wide range of languages. When employing them, it is important to consider the underlying corpus or corpora. Are the texts in the corpora the kind of texts that learners will use on the job or in the pursuit

---

4. The Anthony Lawrence website can be found at https://www.laurenceanthony.net/software/antwordprofiler.

of their language-learning interests? Do they represent written or spoken language? Is it clear where the texts come from? Is it clear when they were created?

Many corpora, like the Russian National Corpus, tend to use a larger number of freely available texts in electronic format, which include a larger number of texts from previous centuries than one might like. In the experience of FSI Russian instructors, *War and Peace* profiled very nicely and yielded the kind of results expected. President Putin's annual press conferences, on the other hand, presented with many words not on the lists, including high numbers of international cognates. This says that word frequency lists and underlying corpora may not have been updated with sufficient numbers of more recent texts or may not include texts that represent the topic set covered in Mr. Putin's press conferences. On the other hand, a student with 9000-word families should be able to read *War and Peace*!

When words in a particular 1000-word family band tend to appear in alphabetical order, it is safe to assume that the underlying corpus is not large enough to sustain at that level. When designing corpora, it is important to set out the principles first. One question will be, how many times does a word need to appear in the corpora in order for it to appear on your list? The more the better. The Russian program at FSI used 50 as the cut point. If a word appeared fewer than 50 times, it was not included in the lists. (Remember that in any given text nearly half of the words will appear only once, so one can say nothing about the frequency of those words.) In order to achieve 50 hits, a corpus of some three million tokens was required.

Since FSI students work in six or seven main topic areas, six or seven sub corpora for each language were chosen. This provided some very important information. If a word appeared in each of the sub corpora a number of times, that word would work nicely in a general frequency list. If the word appeared in only one or two lists, it presented a choice: either throw the word out or create a topic specific word list. The academic word lists created for English would be such lists. Someone training health workers might well want to create a word family frequency list specific to health care or to a topic within the health care domain, and such a sub corpus would support doing that.

A word of caution is due at this point. Program designers can be more than willing to create word lists rather than consulting the corpora. They think they know what needs to be there. So, a lesson on going to the emergency room might include the word *sprain* for situations like, "I think I sprained my ankle." In looking at word frequency lists, however, the word "sprain" appears as a fairly low frequency word.

The main question to be answered when creating word-family frequency lists is whether students can understand or guess the meaning of a word even if they have not encountered it before. If yes, then the presence of that word in a text does not make the text more difficult. If no, it does. In the Nation lists that are supplied with AntWord profiler, *walk, walked, walking, walks* make up a family. *Walkway, Walkman,* and *walkable* are not included in the family. The family for *go* includes *goes, going, gone,* and *went*. Whether to include *went* in the family depends on how likely students are to know that it is the past tense of *go*. In the first week(s) of English, they may not. Later on, they would.

In the national Welsh curriculum, the word "cyngor" (council, advice) is introduced in Chapter 14 of the Introductory course. For a word family list to be used with AntWordProfiler, the entry would include the four consonant mutations: *cyngor, gyngor* (*gair o gyngor*: words of advice), *nghygor* (*fy nghygor*: my advice), *chyngor* (*ymchwiliadau a chyngor*: investigations and advice). To that set of basic forms, one might also add the forms for *advisor*: *cynghorydd, gynghorydd, nghynghorydd, chynghorydd*, and their plurals *cyngorwyr, gyngorwyr, nghyngorwyr,* as well as *chyngorwyr* (councilor/ councilors) since at this point in the course students would have little trouble guessing the meaning even if they had not seen the word previously. The morphological transparency of the relationships among the words makes it possible, and therefore it is necessary to put all of the words in the entry under the head word "cyngor" for the purposes of the AntWord Profiler. Guessing that a learner probably knows the word "cyngor," it might be safe to assume that the learner will have no problem with *cyngor meddyg* (doctor's advice) and should also be able to handle *cyngor sir* (county council).

For languages with many inflections, like Russian, each entry can become quite long. Russian verbs would include the infinitive and the inflected forms. If the perfective/ imperfective pair is obvious, all of the forms for both would be included. One could also add the gerunds and participles and all of their forms. Now we are easily at some 70 or more forms.

There is as much art as linguistics to preparing the word lists. The instructional designer needs to work closely with the teachers and students in order to understand what should and what should not go into a word family list. The most significant consideration is the need to remember that the created lists must help judge the probability that a student will be able to understand a word in context without a tremendous amount of work. Deciding which words become part of the family requires a solid understanding of the learners and a solid understanding of the language. The needs and abilities of the learner are more important to the list than the specific features of the language. The language may have forms for which there is no need to account.

For a number of languages other than English, as seen with the examples from Welsh, the task can be large, especially where no word frequency lists exist. This need to create a word frequency list gives the instructional designer a wonderful opportunity to create precisely the right list which will yield optimal results for the involved learners. Creating word frequency lists may take a considerable amount of time, but it is time well-spent. Nation (2016) laid out the framework for creating word lists, suggesting strategies and requirements for underlying corpora, and reasonable cut off points. It turns out, that creating a reliable list of the most common 3000-word families in a language requires a corpus of 3.5 million tokens. It's a big job, but not an impossible one.

AntWordProfiler has limitations. It does not recognize that two words that look the same may be different. The noun *дорога* (road) and the short form feminine adjective *дорога* (expensive) look exactly the same, and the software cannot tell them apart. Fortunately for this pair, both words are in the first thousand-word list, so the profile will not be off. The instructor may have to help the students here if they are confusing the two words.

AntWordProfiler uses the simplest definition of a word: a group of letters with a space at each end. That causes not insurmountable problems for languages like Thai and Burmese that do not put spaces between words. "I like spicy southern food" in Thai would be ฉันชอบอาหารใต้รสเผ็ด. There is word segmentation software that will split the words apart making it possible to use AntWordProfiler to profile the texts, a question which will be addressed below.

Vietnamese has the opposite problem. Groups of letters in Vietnamese represent the Chinese characters that used to represent them. Thus, if a word had two or three characters, now it has two of three groups of letters. Adventure, thus, is cuộc phiêu lưu, which would be read as three words by the software. This feature of Vietnamese has presented a problem still in search of a solution.

AntWordProfiler also read separable verbs, like "look up," as two words. These can present special problems in English and German and would require the intervention of the instructor when students experience unexpected problems.

Up to this point, we have talked about how the instructor can create precisely the right program for learners. But, as we all know, even the best laid plans often go awry. If a student doesn't do the homework, the student will fail. So, learner behavior must be taken into account.

Learner Responsibilities and Rights

The learner has many responsibilities, the most important of which is to do the reading and the listening. In the real world, however, we know that students, especially the types of adult professionals who often populate training programs at the Distinguished level, have responsibilities and obligations that distract them from their language learning intentions. Many learners have families, kids to take to soccer games, children to be put to bed, meals to prepare, etc. They also have jobs and things they may have to do for their work.[5] And the time for meaningful uninterrupted reading is gone. It is best to devote, especially in the beginning, class time to meaning-focused input.

The student has rights. Daniel Pennac (2015) proposed ten rights, which are condensed here, with commentary based on years of experience at FSI working with adults in distinguished level programs.

The Right Not to Read

One of the few guarantees in a language program is that students who never read will never read, causing major damage to the students' final learning outcomes. However, if on any particular day, a learner doesn't feel like reading, or decides that other demands are more important, then that learner can invoke the right not to read.

---

5. Unique to FSI is the fact that students do have work offices to which they belong and while released from work for language study can sometimes be asked to assist with a task or two, reducing the amount of time available for study.

The Right to Skip

The learner may want to skip long descriptions of nature or episodes in the book that feel irrelevant, and that's okay. That learner probably skips in English, too.

The Right Not to Finish a Book

The rule of fifty (Pearl, 2011) helps here. At about page 50, the reader decides whether the book is worth continuing. If it is not interesting, too difficult, too easy, or in some other way wrong for the reader, the readers can stop reading and move on to the next book.

The Right to Read It Again

Rereading passages, or even whole books, can bring real pleasure. It is a way to see words and constructions over again and may move the activity over into the fluency strand.

The Right to Read Anything

Teachers who thrive on chaos manage this best. Lock-step approaches have a tendency to hold learners from achieving their linguistic potential. Learning to let go is good faculty development.

The Right to Mistake a Book for Real Life

Here is the golden rule! Once the learner has achieved reading and viewing proficiency at the level of fluency that allows being swept away by the materials, getting lost in the adventure, and discovering that it is already 3 o'clock in the morning, the learner is moving into the Distinguished levels of proficiency.

The Right to Read Anywhere

The happiest moment in the meaningful input strand is when learners confess to the teacher that they have become so interested in what they were reading or watching that they took it home and finished it over the weekend. At this point, meaningful input can start to become homework, and learners, if possible, should be allowed to read in favorite venues—the library, a corner, or even outside the classroom on the steps.

The Right to Dip In

The right to dip in. When learners are focused on relevant content, they may want to read portions of a book, not necessarily starting from the very beginning. That is okay, even if not all the students in a group will be reading the same thing.

The Right to Read Aloud

Reading aloud has gotten an unfair bad rap in recent years. The difficulty of reading aloud has frequently been underestimated by instructors. On the other hand, sometimes a text can feel so good that readers want to read it aloud (or even to memorize it—something else that has gotten an unfair bad rap in recent years).

The Right to be Quiet

Of all of Pennac's rights, this is the most challenging for instructors. The learner has the right to quietly process the reading text and not be pushed to defend ideas or answer comprehension questions. In the meaning focused input strand of the training program, the learning is focused on the meaning that is important to individual teachers. They may not have paid attention to the color of Natasha's dress or how many objects were in the drawer. So, what should the teacher ask when the student finishes reading a book? "How did you like it?" "What would you like to read next?"

The ten rights of the reader place the student in the driver's seat. When the materials are interesting, relevant, and at level to the student, the student is more likely to do the homework. When the student has the right to stop reading, or even not to read, the requirement that materials be interesting becomes critical. Neither the instructional designer nor the teacher tells the student what to read. They help guide the student toward materials that will hold their interests.

Conclusion

A properly constructed program at the Distinguished level may feel chaotic for experienced teachers. The learners in the program are most likely reading different books, watching different videos, and preparing different oral presentations. Specialists designing training programs and the teachers delivering them will have spent considerable time reading and evaluating materials to be able to answer the question, "What should the class read/watch/talk about next?" To answer that question, the instructors need to know their students well since the materials need to be interesting (to the learner), relevant (especially in the context of the learner's onward assignment or endeavors), and at level.

Not everyone agrees. Nation and Waring (2019) do not support the idea that learning materials should always be interesting. Clifford (2018) does not support the idea that learning and assessment materials need to be relevant to the learner's onward assignment.

While learners at the basic levels generally start out with the same lack of language-specific schemata and therefore have similar needs (accounting, of course, for those who are heritage learners or have studied other languages, perhaps even from the same family), each learner at the Distinguished level is unique (Mueller, 2003) in a number or respects: the specific vocabulary and grammar they have acquired, their now-honed approaches to language learning, their use of strategies, and the manner in which they have reached the Distinguished level, or close to it. Learners need feedback and guidance but may not need much in terms of instruction in the traditional sense although most report needing and wanting some direct instruction for specific items, particularly those in the area of cultural differences (Leaver & Atwell, 2002). Most significantly, learners working toward the Distinguished level need to process and produce massive amounts of text; for that they may upon occasion need guidance from instructors who have a more comprehensive knowledge of what texts exist and which texts might best serve their immediate and long-term needs. And sometimes, learners just simply do not know what they do not know, interpreting linguistic and cultural phenomena from an English-centric point of view, and need both explanation and transformative experiences designed by instructors and program managers to push them up into the Distinguished realm.

References

Anon. (2023). *Just the right book*. Downloaded from https://childrenslibrarylady.com/just-right-book/.

Anon. (2023). *Zipf's and Heap's Law*. Downloaded from https://www.ccs.neu.edu/home/ekanou/ISU535.09X2/Handouts/Review_Material/zipfslaw.pdf.

Clifford, R. (2018). *Test validation for people with proficiency standards*. Downloaded from https://www.govtilr.org/Calendars/Clifford.pdf.

Doughty, C., & Williams, J. (1998). *Focus on form in classroom second language acquisition*. New York: Cambridge University Press.

Franke, J. (2020). *Pursuing Distinguished speaking proficiency with adult foreign language learners: A case study*. Doctoral dissertation, American College of Education.

Hacking, J., & Tschirner, E. (2017). The contribution of vocabulary knowledge to reading proficiency: The case of college Russian. *Foreign Language Annals* 50 (3): 500-518.

Hu, H.M., & Nation, P. (2000). What vocabulary size is required to read unsimplified texts. *Reading in a Foreign Language,* 8, 689-696.

Interagency Language Roundtable (ILR). (August 2, 2022). *Skill level descriptions*. Downloaded from https://www.govtilr.org/Skills/ILRscale4.htm.

IRIS. 2023. *What is the average reading speed in various languages?* Downloaded from https://irisreading.com.

Krashen, S. D. (1997). *Foreign language education: The easy way*. Culver City, California: Language Education Association.

Leaver, B. L., & Atwell, S. A. (2002). Preliminary qualitative findings from a study of the processes leading to Advanced Professional Proficiency (ILR-4). In B. L. Leaver & B. S. Shekhtman, eds. *Developing professional-level foreign language proficiency*. (260-279). Cambridge, UK: Cambridge University Press.

Lichtman, K., & Van Patten, B. 2021. Was Krashen right? Forty years later. *Foreign Language Annals* 54 (2): 283-305.

Ljashevskaja, O., & Sharov, S. (2009). *Novyi chastotnyj slovar' russkoj leksiki*. Downloaded from https://en.wiktionary.org/wiki.

McLeod, S. (2023). *Memory stages: Encoding and retrieval*. Downloaded from Simply Psychology: https://simplypsychology.org/memory/html.

Milton, J. (2009). *Measuring second language vocabulary acquisition*. Bristol, UK: Multilingual Matters.

Mueller, C. (2003). Tracing the steps of the successful multilingual: A synopsis. *Journal for Distinguished Language Studies* 1(1): 51-58.

Nation, P. (2013). *What should every EFL teacher know?* Korea: Compass Publishing.

Nation, P. (2014). *Is it possible to learn enough vocabulary from extensive reading?* Downloaded from https://www.youtube.com/watch?v=GpsVp95Wu_E.

Nation, P. (2016). *Making and using word lists for language learning and testing.* Amsterdam: John Benjamins Publishing Company.

Nation, P. (2017). *Applying the four Strands: Dr. Paul Nation speaks to FSI on language learning.* Downloaded from https://www.youtube.com/watch?v=A-mA5jFBF0U&t=1480s.

Nation, I. S. P., & Waring, R. (2020). *Teaching extensive reading in another language.* New York and London: Routledge.

Pearl, N. (February 4, 2011). Nancy Pearl's Rule of 50 for dropping a bad book. *The Globe and Mail.*

Pennac, D. (2015). *The rights of the reader.* Sara Ardizzone, translator. Somerville, MA: Candlewick.

Tokarczuk, O. (2022). *The books of Jacob.* Jennifer Croft, translator. New York: Riverhead Books.

TORFL. (2023). *Test of Russian as a Foreign Language.* Downloaded from https://torflrussian.com.

About the Author

James Bernhardt, Ph. D., is retired from the Foreign Service Institute where he served first as Russian Language Training Supervisor and then as Department Chair of Asian and African Languages. He has written articles for various publications and most recently a co-authored piece with Betty Lou Leaver and Christine Campbell for a co-edited volume (Oxford et al.), *Peacebuilding in Language Education.*

Roadmaps to Distinguished Speaking Proficiency

Jack Franke, Defense Language Institute (USA)

Abstract

Although study abroad is viewed in the United States as *sine qua non*, the study abroad experience is not a panacea to achieve distinguished foreign language speaking proficiency. This study attempts to uncover how persistence, study abroad, motivation, and learner autonomy play into the pursuit of distinguished speaking proficiency. Using the theoretical framework of complexity theory and phenomenological design, the study utilizes interviews of four educators at an institute in the western United States as the primary instrument of data collection. This study investigates the roadmaps which successful foreign language educators have utilized to achieve distinguished speaking proficiency through interviews and documentary research. Data analysis of interviews with the participants reveals distinguished speaking proficiency was a highly personal pursuit, characterized by different motivations based on the choice of a foreign language, engagement in the target culture, grit, and time. Overall, the participants were highly self-efficacious learners, many married to foreign-speaking spouses, who spent extended periods in the foreign culture and community. The study provides possible roadmaps for students and for educators who wish to achieve near-native speaking proficiency in a foreign language.

Keywords: distinguished proficiency, grit, study abroad, motivation.

The demand for linguistic expertise continues to grow in the United States (Rivers & Brecht, 2018). In 2017, 332,727 students from the United States went on study abroad programs around the world; 70% of these students traveled to Western Europe or Latin America (Institute of International Education, 2018). Based on the calculations of Rivers and Brecht (2018), the United States requires over 16,000 experts with distinguished levels of language proficiency in national security, business, and diplomacy. Although the Language Flagship Program has successfully achieved superior level and above in critical languages with speaking proficiency, the numbers of highly proficient speakers are severely inadequate for America's increasing demand (Davidson, Garas, & Lekic, 2016). In the past, America has often counted on heritage communities and native speakers to fill the majority of positions requiring distinguished proficiency (Rivers & Brecht, 2018). Despite the necessity of linguistic expertise, a perceived ceiling effect in American classrooms circumscribes students to upper-intermediate levels (Rifkin, 2005). Unfortunately, the lack of bilingualism in the United States, combined with a dearth of college graduates attaining superior levels of language proficiency, leaves a vacuum in the United States for distinguished-level linguists.

There is a misunderstanding prevalent in the United States that functional proficiency is sufficient—most often termed as "survival language." As noted by numerous scholars, advanced-level proficiency is the minimum level for communicative purposes in numerous professions—social work, medicine, human resources—to name a few (Rifkin, 2005; Swender, 2003). The importance of the problem lies in the fact that a need exists in the United States for highly proficient linguists in international business, diplomacy, and national security, as well as medicine, social work, and numerous other professions (Leaver, 2003; McGinn, 2015). Those impacted by this problem include educators who are uninformed about the requirements to attain near-native proficiency and students who possess no roadmap to these levels. Many studies have successfully quantified lower levels of speaking proficiency; conversely, there is a dearth of literature on superior or distinguished proficiency, with the exception of Kagan, Kubler, Walker, Yu, and Leaver. To understand how these outliers achieved near-native proficiency, this study sought to ascertain how some distinguished foreign language (FL) speakers have achieved this level of proficiency. In an examination of distinguished FL speakers, several common denominators were revealed: study abroad, motivation, strategies for success, and persistence.

Theoretical Framework

Complexity Theory (CT) is transdisciplinary and well-suited for research involving many fields, including second language acquisition, and is the framework employed in this study (Larsen-Freeman, 2015). Complexity Theory has served as a framework within applied linguistics in order to examine the language learning process with a new lens. Whereas traditional SLA theorists view the learner as a static entity often defined by proficiency, CT examines the learner as an aggregate of the mind, body, and environment (Nishino & Atkinson, 2015). CT was relevant to the given research because there are at least eight features in the complexity theory: 1) adaptive, 2) affordances, 3) chaotic, 4) complex, 5) dynamic, 6) nonlinear, 7) open, and 8) self-organizing (Larsen-Freeman, 2015).

Although CT has been used to explain phenomena in the sciences i.e., how a flock of birds emerges from the interaction of individual birds, the interdisciplinarity of near-native speaking proficiency warrants an examination of components necessary for its genesis (Larsen-Freeman, 2015). Van Lier (2000) makes explicit the relationship between unpredictability and chaos/complex ways of thought: for example, an L2 learner put in an unfamiliar situation with a customs agent in the foreign country, or refugees compelled to migrate to another country. Complexity theory is most apropos in regard to self-efficacious learners: the L2 learner has moved from pedagogical to andragogical approaches in SLA, the motivation is high, the affective filter is low, and the student avails himself of time in the L2 community or study abroad. The proximal goals build on one another while simultaneously striving for the distal goal. Although attaining next-higher levels of proficiency may present a straight-line progression of advancement over time, achieving superior and then distinguished proficiency require increasing longer periods of time—especially in productive skills.

Review of the Literature

Study Abroad

At some point in the continuum of second language acquisition (SLA), many foreign language learners choose to leave the foreign-language classroom and immerse themselves in a study abroad context where the L2 is spoken natively and predominantly, normally with a planned curriculum and frequently with a host family (Collentine, 2009). In order to aggregate findings in the field of study abroad, the research is focused on those aspects which lead to advanced levels of L2 speaking proficiency namely: intercultural competence, learner identity, socio- and intercultural competence, linguistic gains, duration of immersion experiences, and the development of fluency, accuracy, and automaticity. The sheer magnitude of all the components of a distinguished speaker in the L2 is vast; the hallmark of a near-native speaker is the ability to shift in registers, speculate on highly abstract topics, support an opinion at a high level, give both formal and informal speeches, and interpret (Interagency Language Roundtable, 2012). The abovementioned topics address components of study abroad which were relevant to the given research.

Study abroad (SA) is a vehicle by which students are immersed in the foreign language and culture for short-term or long-term periods. The International Institute of Education (2018) reported over 300,000 American students participated in study abroad for academic credit in the 2016-2017 academic year. Students take part in SA not only for language and culture, but also for internships, social and volunteer services, and experiential learning (Toner, 2019). Apart from language proficiency and cultural gains, students develop numerous other soft skills, including intercultural competence, adaptability, tolerance, dealing with ambiguity, interpersonal awareness, and cross-cultural understanding. In order to achieve near-native proficiency, Van Lier (2000) drew our attention to the necessity of these soft skills and competencies in adaptation as an L2 learner.

Critical Period Hypothesis

Critical period hypothesis (CPH) posits the ability to acquire full or native-like fluency is possible up unto the point of puberty (Lenneberg, 1967; Moyer, 2018). Due to neurobiological limits and electro-chemical changes in the brain (plasticity, lateralization), Lenneberg emphasized the impact of late exposure on first and second language acquisition, especially on phonology (Moyer, 2018). According to Lenneberg, pre-pubertal children acquire language in both hemispheres of the brain. Other scholars (Vanhove,

2013; Moyer, 2018) propose the critical period as a range from infancy to late teens or as late as 22 years of age. While there are disagreements in the exact time of the critical period, scholars agree brain changes result in a decline in the ability for language learning (Strid, 2017; Vanhove, 2013).

Language gains during study abroad. Research on study abroad strongly demonstrated language proficiency gains, especially in L2 oral proficiency (Baker-Smemoe et al., 2014; Brecht, Davidson, & Ginsberg, 1993; Davidson, 2010; Di Silvio et al., 2014; Magnan & Back, 2007). Leonard and Shea (2017) emphasized speaking proficiency was not evenly distributed across all dimensions. For example, in the assessment of oral proficiency, the person tested is evaluated on global linguistic skills, sociocultural competence, grammatical control (accuracy), lexical control, delivery, and fluency. Recent studies have examined the granularity of speaking proficiency and determined students with higher L2 linguistic knowledge, schemata, and L2 processing speed achieved higher gains and could address topics requiring a higher cognitive load during study abroad, which corroborated hypotheses expressed by Brecht et al. (1993) and Magnan and Back (2007). These findings support the results of Davidson (2010) insofar as those students who reached superior levels were already at advanced high or superior before the beginning of the study abroad Flagship program. Indeed, Leonard and Shea (2017) found a correlation between students who had background knowledge of the language before the SA experience and the ability to engage in more complex syntactical and lexical constructions. These results indicated students with a foundation in grammar and vocabulary may possess more cognitive resources which allow these speakers to enhance text type and accuracy in the L2.

Apart from mere study abroad, the ability to experience a homestay with a host family in the target language is often viewed as the ideal environment. Di Silvio et al. (2014) found correlations between homestays and oral proficiency gains, as well as satisfaction with the students' learning. In empirical research in these languages—Arabic, Chinese, French, Spanish, and Russian—nuanced differences were noted based on variables such as gender, age, intercultural sensitivity, personality, affective filter, and social networks (Baker-Smemoe et al., 2014; Di Silvio et al., 2014). Watson and Wolfel (2015) suggested students be matched with a program conducive to strengths and addressed four areas of improvement: 1) addressing strategies to maximize proficiency gains, 2) during-immersion progress checks for reflection, 3) encouraging more participation via community service, travel, and family activities, and 4) comparing results with alignment of the host institutions' effectiveness. These implications coincided with the findings of Baker-Smemoe et al. (2014); social networks were indeed the most essential element to achieve speaking gains during the study abroad.

Second language identity and persistence. To achieve near-native proficiency, a student undergoes a metamorphosis in self-identity. At the level of distinguished proficiency, a learner speaks succinctly and often uses cultural and historical references. Depending on the language, culture may be reflected in a shift from a monochronic mindset to a polychronic one, or the use of Koranic language to reflect social mores. The ability to shift in registers in a culturally appropriate manner along with deeply embedded cultural references are the hallmark of an L2 speaker at distinguished proficiency (ACTFL, 2012). Block (2007) defined identity as the negotiation of meanings "at the crossroads of past, present, and future" (p.27). Learners are shaped by the worldview and schemata along a continuum, where learners rely on past experiences but are shaped by future ones, resulting in discord and ambivalence from competing identities. Similarly, Roshandel, Ghonsooly, and Ghanizadeh (2018) reviewed Lambert's model of subtractive and additive bilingualism, where learners choose to learn a foreign language, resulting in additive consequences. For ESL learners, the discord corresponds to the external desire to learn the majority language; for L2 learners, the ambivalence may arise in conflicts of core values between L1 and L2 and may impact self-efficacy as well. Through pragmatic and sociocultural competence gains during SA, the learner progresses from advanced to superior and ultimately distinguished proficiency. In instances where there is no past knowledge or situations which vastly differ from L1—in this study, English—this conflict with identity may occur. Franke (2019) conducted case studies with English language learners and one respondent stated:

> I'd always defined myself as a German dude and I told everyone, "Hey, I'm from Germany, that's me. I'm the German guy." And I used that to explain away other idiosyncrasies and personality traits. So to come into contact with Germans my age in high school and find that I'm not able to communicate with them like peers and that I'm not part of that community anymore was really painful for me actually. (Franke, 2019, p. 4)

Further, conflicts resulting from social mores in the target culture may destabilize one's self-perception and a new emotional or moral balance is necessary for harmony (Kinginger, 2013, p. 341).

Pedagogy, andragogy, and heutagogy. In learner autonomy, reviewing the origins of these concepts is essential and how pedagogy, andragogy, heutagogy play a role in second language acquisition. When a baby or child is engaged in the negotiation of information and knowledge, this aspect is *pedagogy* (Blaschke, 2012). Until Freire (1970) challenged the notions of a student as an empty vessel waiting to be filled, the "sage on the stage" was *de rigeur*. Later, self-determined learning, or andragogy, was accepted as learners were perceived as more capable of using the skills and knowledge to deal with unfamiliar situations independently. Although andragogy is typically found in adult learners, mature high school students with intrinsic motivation may certainly exhibit self-directness and actively engage in individual needs (Blaschke, 2012). Learners began to cultivate knowledge, facilitate knowledge, were intrinsically motivated, and exhibited a focus on life-centered goals (Halupa & Still, 2014). This concept of self-directed and student-centered learning is referred to as *andragogy* (Blaschke, 2012). Recently, flipped classrooms and e-portfolios are two examples of andragogical approaches to learning, and self-directed learning and self-assessment have been demonstrated as beneficial both in K-12 and adult language learners (Halupa & Still, 2014; Jafarigohar, Sharifi, & Soleimani, 2017). The final concept is *heutagogy*, where learning is self-directed and requires minimal to no assistance from an instructor or mentor (Blaschke, 2012). In online and distance education, heutagogy is ubiquitous because of the inherent nature of this modality (Blaschke, 2012).

To best illustrate the differences between pedagogy, andragogy, and heutagogy from a linguistic perspective, an analogy of a car may be utilized (Blaschke, 2012; Halupa & Still, 2014). In pedagogy, the L2 learner is in the passenger seat or sitting in the back of a car. The learner may or may not be aware of how the car is being propelled, or what the driver is doing while driving. In andragogy, the student has a learner's permit and is periodically driving the car with the instructor as a guide on the side. There is an intrinsic motivation to "get behind the wheel" and take charge of the learning process. To drive to school or work, the motivation is intensified in an instrumental fashion. The student is attuned to conditions and receives input from time to time to cultivate knowledge. In heutagogy, the student is driving on the German Autobahn at night—at 150 miles per hour. In this scenario, the student has a license to drive, has driven alone on highways, and is experienced driving at high speeds at nighttime. As with weather conditions on the Autobahn, contextual situations may play a factor in learning.

In heutagogy, the L2 learner is engaged in double-loop learning: not only is the learner considering problems and solutions, but the learner is simultaneously engaged in questioning his value system and actions (Blaschke, 2012). The student is examining both competencies and capabilities in a form of self-reflection. In a process of conscious self-assessment, the L2 learner demonstrates self-efficacy, communication skills, creativity, and positive values (Blaschke, 2012). Examples of heutagogical approaches include learner contracts and learner-directed questions in a flexible curriculum (Blaschke, 2012). During a heutagogically-designed SA experience, the student is engaged in self-reflection on a continual basis. Until mastery is achieved on a given task, the L2 learner remains focused. When the student encounters lexical breakdown on a task or a probe to a higher speaking level (as a stretch objective), the learner seeks to scaffold her learning with a mentor or teacher. In distance learning modalities, the student is compelled to channel energies toward distal or proximal goals—normally without instructor control. The student connects with peers and colleagues to seek solutions to inevitable challenges as affordances in self-determined learning activities. Self-assessment is generally utilized in heutagogical approaches to learning by extemporaneous speeches and other tasks raised to distinguished proficiency levels—sometimes based on the receptions of his/her native interlocutors.

Methodology

This qualitative case study design examined the strategies adult language learners employ in order to achieve near-native speaking proficiency. The setting for the research was an educational institution in the Western United States. The participants included professional educators who are near-native speakers of Chinese, Spanish, and Russian. These participants are educators in both undergraduate and graduate foreign language programs. The rationale for using case study research is three-fold: 1) the main research question addressed "why" or "how" questions; 2) the researcher had little to no control over behaviors; and 3) the focus of the study was on contemporary phenomena (Yin, 2018). Yin (2018) noted the main focus is on decisions in a case study: the rationale for taking decisions, how the decisions were implemented, and what was the result.

The case study sample size consisted of four participants who took part in two interviews each. Creswell and Creswell (2018) noted that case studies should be based on four to five cases (p. 186). The primary investigator (PI) conducted all the interviews. The interviews addressed the aforementioned themes, with embedded units of analysis for each theme. The interviews lasted for approximately two hours, and there were two iterations for each participant, for a total of four hours. The interviewees are all educators in an educational institution in the Western United States and have all taught several years in their specific languages, namely: Chinese, Russian, and Spanish. Yin (2018) noted interviews are "one of the most important sources of case study evidence" (p. 110). Creswell (2014) reiterated the fact that case studies are a method of inquiry to perform an in-depth analysis of an activity of one or more individuals (p. 14). The ability for English native speakers to achieve distinguished speaking proficiency in the L2 qualified as such an activity or phenomenon. Through case studies, patterns of the participants' strategies to become near-native speakers in the foreign language were evidenced.

The purpose of this case study was to examine the lived experiences of some educators who were able to achieve distinguished speaking proficiency in the target language. The study is focused on production skills, namely speaking, rather than literacy or receptive skills. Since the literature on speaking modalities at the near-native level was sparse, a description of the lived experiences of those who have achieved distinguished proficiency in the L2 was warranted. This phenomenological case study was guided by two research questions.

Research Question One: How do the participants describe the ability to achieve distinguished proficiency? The question was designed to capture data and insights into the educators who became near-native speakers in a foreign language. The participants shared experiences and insights to achieve extremely high levels of speaking proficiency. Additionally, the participants related stories which demonstrated their tenacity, persistence, motivation, and determination to excel. An awareness of these traits may serve educators and students alike whose aim is to achieve distinguished speaking proficiency.

Research Question Two: What strategies did the participants employ to achieve such high proficiency levels? The question explored the paths each participant took in order to become a near-native speaker in a foreign language. Participants revealed fascinating and important insights into overcoming obstacles, as well as transitions from advanced to superior and ultimately distinguished proficiency. The common thread among participants was language learning is not linear, and each participant encountered different challenges in a highly personalized way. The findings encountered from the research question may provide further justification for tailored instruction geared to each FL student—especially at advanced levels.

Roadmaps to Proficiency

After a review of the participants' transcripts, the roadmaps to distinguished proficiency were varied and became quite salient. The mere fact of applying effort to talent in developing foreign language skills or applying effort to these newly-developed skills for achievement only paints half the picture. Each participant demonstrated grit by overcoming obstacles on the path to near-native proficiency, and a visual display of each participant's roadmap is warranted. In total, there are four roadmaps: a "traditional" student model, an undergraduate student model, an intensive immersion model, and a complete study abroad model. The first roadmap of a "traditional" student is depicted in Figure 4.

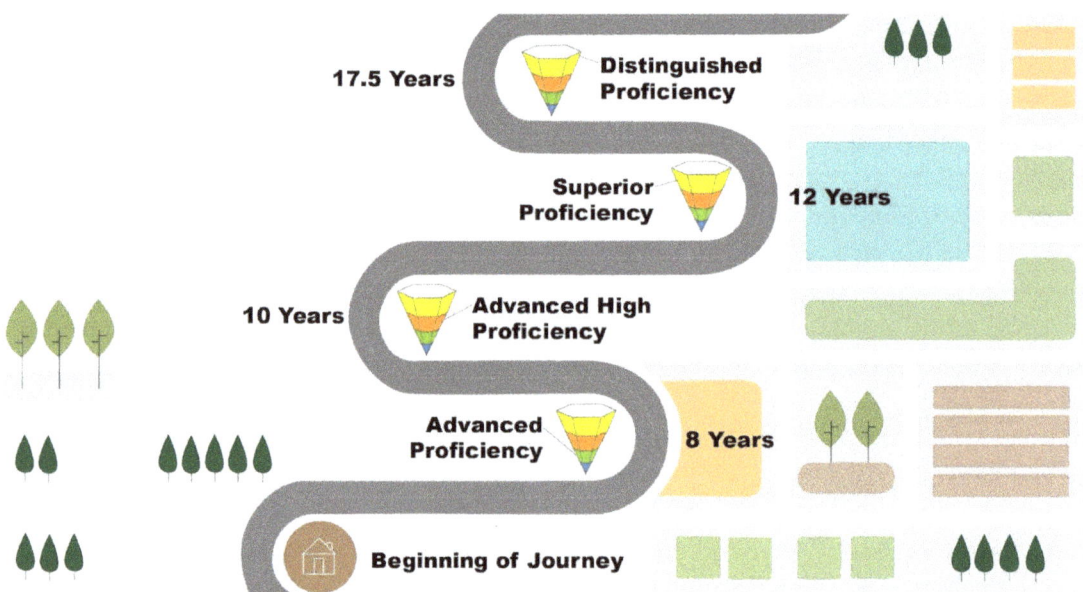

Figure 4. Roadmap to Distinguished Proficiency (Type 1 – "Traditional Student" Model).

The first model represents a student who began foreign language studies in junior high school. As told by the participant, the foreign language teachers were average and the input was inferior. After high school, the participant went on the first study abroad experience and realized the proficiency skills were lacking. The participant matriculated as a foreign language major undergraduate student. The participant went on two more study abroad opportunities, including an internship. Upon graduation from college, the participant had achieved advanced level speaking proficiency. The student was invited to teach the foreign language and actively began a graduate program. During graduate school, in addition to teaching duties, the participant went on an additional study abroad program. The participant galvanized culture, literature, and language during graduate school. Upon completion of the graduate degree, the participant had achieved superior mid proficiency and began teaching the language intensively. Over the next five years the participant was responsible for instruction and curriculum development in advanced FL programs. During this period the educator taught students to superior proficiency in all modalities, focusing on extended discourse, abstract topics, register shifts, and hypothesis. Additionally, the participant married a foreign language-speaking spouse and engaged in high-level language usage with erudite native speaking colleagues. This milieu, both at work and at home, propelled the participant to distinguished level proficiency. The next roadmap depicts a model of an undergraduate student in Figure 5.

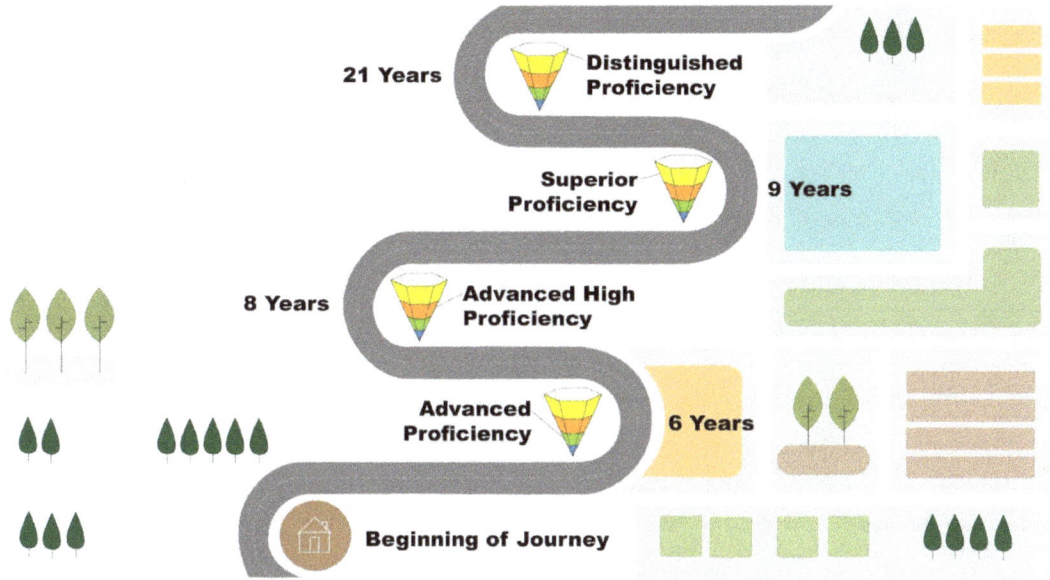

Figure 5. Roadmap to Distinguished Proficiency (Type 2 – Undergraduate Student Model).

The second model represents a student who began foreign language studies in an undergraduate program. Based on interviews with the participant, the educator wanted to study a less-commonly taught language (LCTL). After the practicum, the student graduated from the undergraduate program at an intermediate high proficiency. Wanting to speak the language well, the participant continued the foreign language in a graduate program. During graduate school, the participant studied abroad and reached advanced proficiency. The participant continued in a doctoral program and again studied abroad in an academic year program. While in the doctoral program, the participant achieved distinguished proficiency. Later, the participant taught the foreign language in undergraduate programs and led study abroad programs. The combination of extensive doctoral courses, teaching at the advanced level, and strong phonology instruction pushed the participant to distinguished proficiency. In Figure 6, the next roadmap demonstrates a fully intensive model.

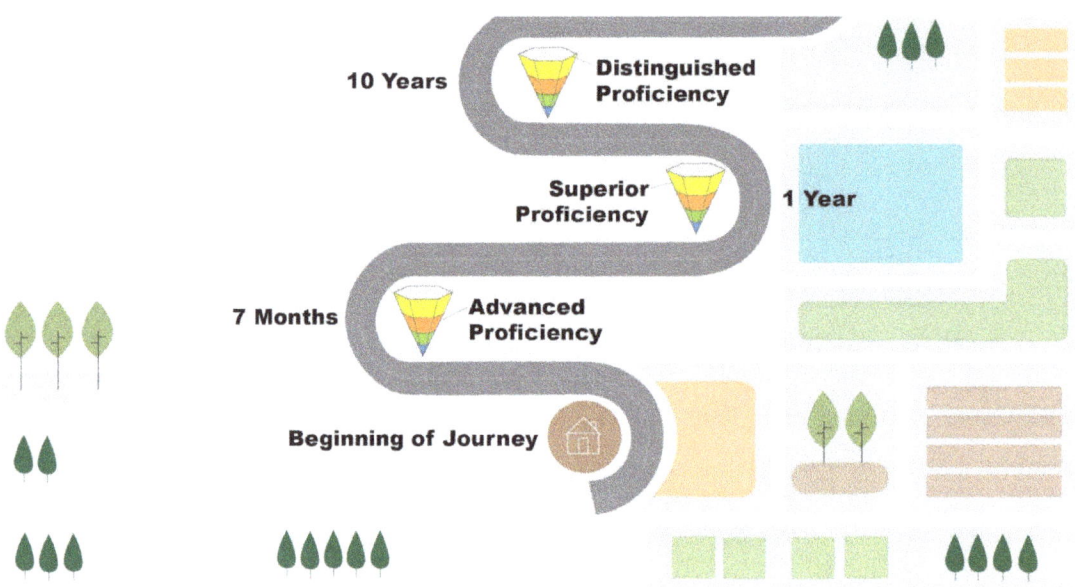

Figure 6. Roadmap to Distinguished Proficiency (Type 3 – Intensive Immersion Model).

The third model represents a student who achieved foreign language proficiency solely in intensive instruction. The participant noted previous study of a foreign language aided in additional language study. While in a year-long intensive program, the participant achieved advanced speaking proficiency after only seven months. After one year, the participant achieved superior proficiency in all modalities—reading, listening, and speaking proficiency. The participant continued graduate-level studies in another year-long intensive program, as well as three years in-country. At this stage, the participant had achieved superior high proficiency. Additionally, the participant matriculated in a graduate program--again in an intensive environment—which propelled the participant to distinguished level proficiency. In Figure 7, the last roadmap depicts a model of a fully study abroad student.

The fourth model represents a student who achieved distinguished language proficiency in study abroad instruction. After graduation from college, the participant chose to move to the target country. The participant taught English and simultaneously studied the foreign language. After two years in-country, the student achieved advanced speaking proficiency. At the four-year mark the participant achieved superior level proficiency. At this point, the participant taught content courses in the target language and married a foreign-language spouse. The participant began a translation bureau with the spouse and achieved superior plus proficiency (ILR 3+) after eight years. Wanting to improve translation and interpretation skills, the participant matriculated into graduate school. After two years in the graduate program and an additional year in-country, the participate broke the ceiling at the superior level into distinguished proficiency.

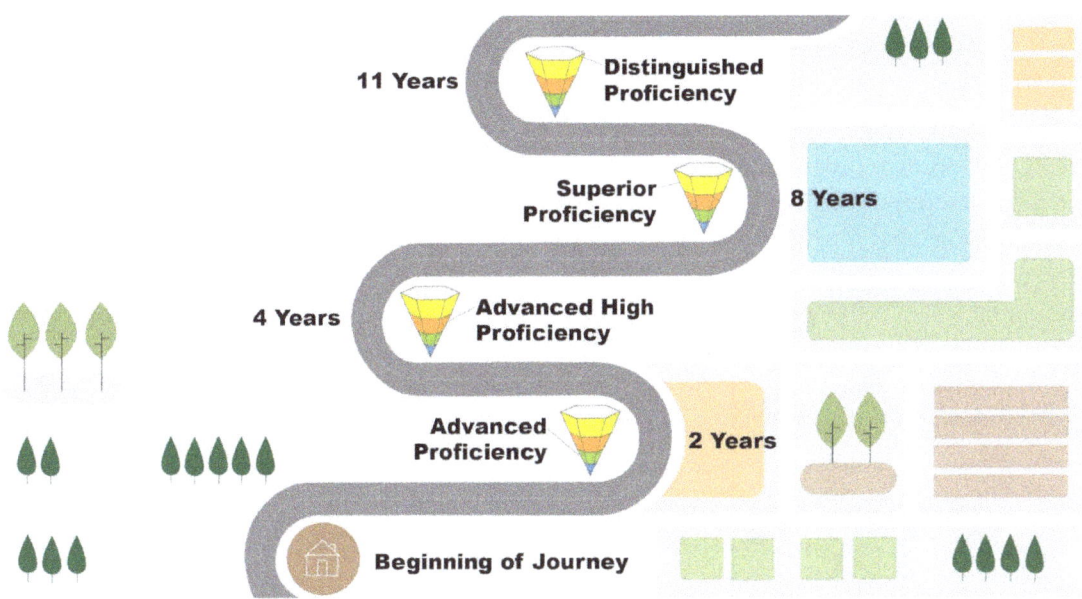

Figure 7. Roadmap to Distinguished Proficiency (Type 4 – Full Overseas Model).

Results

Key findings clearly demonstrated distinguished foreign-language speakers are not a homogeneous group nor can a single roadmap be devised in a linear fashion. In fact, the case studies revealed no two profiles were alike, and the path from beginning to distinguished FL speaker depends on the environment, time in country, motivation, and determination. The experiences described by the participants address Research Question 1, which was to explore the phenomena of distinguished speaking proficiency among foreign language educators. Research Question 2 posed the question of strategies and roadmaps to near-native proficiency and how these strategies enabled the participants to achieve the goal. The responses to Research Question 2 raised issues on the Critical Period Hypothesis (CPH) specifically and revealed individual roadmaps to distinguished proficiency. Since each of the participants achieved near-native distinguished proficiency, puberty cannot be the only determinant of native or near-native fluency. Optimal input, neural maturation, behavioral maturation, and aptitude all play a role in ultimate attainment (Hakuta, 2001; Hartshorne et al., 2018; Moyer, 2018; Strid, 2017; Vanhove, 2013). The roadmaps—although not a hypothesis tested in grounded theory—suggest foreign language students pursuing near-native proficiency may need to introspectively actualize individual roadmaps based on myriad factors such as self-efficacy, maturation, determination, study abroad, and time. Each of the participants demonstrated persistence, for the shortest time period was 10 years, and the longest time period was 21 years. Data suggested participants had high self-awareness, self-efficacy, strategies personalized to one's own goals, and motivation to achieve distinguished proficiency.

Findings

The findings of the study demonstrate the participants' commitment and grit to attain near-native proficiency. Greater numbers of distinguished FL experts are necessary to meet current and future demand in the marketplace. Along with the study, the literature suggested a need to increase programs—both nationally and locally—which may increase the nation's need for FL experts (Davidson et al., 2016; Leaver, 2003; McGinn, 2015; Rivers & Brecht, 2018). The research study identified the phenomena of distinguished proficiency among educators in northern California. Language experts are needed for education, business, diplomacy, and the government. The responsibility of future leaders includes a systematic development of FL programs which enhance and increase greater quantities of near-native FL experts.

Conclusion

The study examined the lived experience of four brilliant, distinguished, foreign language educators in northern California. The research included a small sample of near-native FL speakers of the thousands who have engaged in the intricacies and complexities of distinguished proficiency in the United States. Complexity Theory (CT) provided the framework to unweave the aspects of grit, persistence, determination, automaticity, and heutagogy to achieve near-native proficiency. Globalization has expanded the need for near-native speakers in many sectors of society. The principal investigator is hopeful that leaders in foreign language education—at the national level through policy and language associations—examine the study, reflect on the participants' voices, and consider how the nation can enhance and increase the number of distinguished foreign language speakers.

In a review of the research questions and responses, participants exhibited persistence, tenacity, grit, motivation, and determination. Educators can encourage these traits in students. Whether in a K-12 setting or with adult learners, educators can challenge students to "stretch themselves" on tasks where there are clear deficiencies. Formative feedback, formally or informally, may provide the mechanism to achieve Distinguished Language Proficiency. The study provided evidence of the necessity to establish robust FL programs—both in the United States and abroad—which should increase the number of distinguished speakers. The increase of dual language and baccalaureate programs is a start; further, encouragement and financial support for less-commonly taught languages are essential for national defense, diplomacy, and America's role in the global marketplace.

References

ACTFL. (2012). *ACTFL proficiency guidelines 2012*. Retrieved from https:// actfl.org/publications/guidelines-and-manuals/actfl-proficiency-guidelines-2012/english/speaking.

Baker-Smemoe, W., Dewey, D., Bown, J., & Martinsen, R. (2014). Variables affecting L2 gains during study abroad. *Foreign Language Annals 47*(3): 464-486. https://doi.org/10.1111/flan.12093

Blaschke, L. M. (2012). Heutagogy and lifelong learning: A review of heutagogical practice and self-determined learning. *International Review of Research in Open and Distance Learning 13*(1): 56–71. https://doi.org/10.19173/irrodl.v13i1.1076.

Block, D. (2007). The rise of identity in SLA research: Post Firth and Wagner (1997). *Modern Language Journal 91*: 863-876.

Brecht, R. D., Davidson, D., & Ginsberg, R. B. (1993). *Predictors of foreign language gain during study abroad*. NFLC Occasional Papers. Washington, DC: National Foreign Language Center.

Collentine, J. (2009). Study abroad research: Findings, implications, and future directions. In M. H. Long, & C. J. Doughty (Eds.) *The handbook of language teaching* (pp. 218-233). https://doi:10.1002/9781444315783.ch13.

Creswell, J. W. (2014). *Research design: Qualitative, quantitative, and mixed methods approaches*. Thousand Oaks, CA: Sage.

Creswell, J. W., & Creswell, J. D. (2018). *Research design: Qualitative, quantitative, and mixed methods approaches*. Thousand Oaks, CA: Sage.

Davidson, D. E. (2010). Study abroad: When, how long, and with what results? New data from the Russian front. *Foreign Language Annals, 43*(1): 6-26. https://doi:10.1111/j.1944-9720.2010.01057.x.

Davidson, D., Garas, N., & Lekic, M. (2016). Assessing language proficiency and intercultural development in the overseas immersion context. In D. Murphy & K. Evans-Romaine (Eds.) *Exploring the U.S. language flagship program: Professional competence in a second language by graduation* (pp. 156-176) Bristol, UK: Multilingual Matters.

Di Silvio, F., Donovan, A., & Malone, M. (2014). The effect of study abroad homestay placements: Participant perspectives and oral proficiency gains. *Foreign Language Annals 47*: 168-188.

Franke, J. (2019). *Case studies on self-efficacy in second language acquisition*. Unpublished manuscript, Indianapolis, IN: American College of Education.

Hakuta, K. (2001). *A critical period for second language acquisition*. In D. Bailey, J. Bruer, F. Simmons, & J. W. Lichtman (Eds.), *Critical thinking about critical periods* (pp.193-205). Baltimore, MD: Paul H. Brooks Publishing.

Halupa, C., & Still, A. (2014). Pedagogy, andragogy and heutagogy. In C. Halupa (Ed.), *Transformative curriculum design in health sciences education*. https://doi.org/10.4018/978-1-4666-8571-0.ch005.

Hartshorne, J., Tennenbaum, J., & Pinker, S. (2018). A critical period for second language acquisition: Evidence from 2/3 million English speakers. https://*doi*.org/10.1016/j.cognition.2018.04.007.

Interagency Language Roundtable. (2012). *Description of proficiency levels*. Retrieved from http://govtilr.org/Skills/ILRscale.htm.

International Institute of Education. (2018). Data. Retrieved from https://www.iie.org/en/Research-and-Insights/Open-Doors/Data.

Jafarigohar, M., Sharifi, M., & Soleimani, H. (2017). E-portfolio evaluation and vocabulary learning: Moving from pedagogy to andragogy. *British Journal of Educational Technology 48*(6): 1441–1450. https://doi.org/10.1111/bjet.12479.

Kinginger, C. (2013), Identity and language learning in study abroad. *Foreign Language Annals 46*: 339-358. https://doi:10.1111/flan.12037.

Larsen-Freeman, D. (2015). Complexity theory. In B. VanPatten & J. Williams (Eds.), *Theories in second language acquisition: An introduction* (pp. 227-244). New York, NY: Routledge.

Leaver, B. (2003). *Achieving native-like second-language proficiency: A catalogue of critical factors*. Salinas, CA: CDLC Imprints.

Lenneberg, E. (1967). *Biological foundations of language*. New York, NY: John Wiley & Sons.

Leonard, K. R., & Shea, C. E. (2017). L2 speaking development during study abroad: Fluency, accuracy, complexity, and underlying cognitive factors. *Modern Language Journal 101*: 179-193. https://doi.org/10.1111/modl.12382.

Magnan, S., & Back, M. (2007). Social interaction and linguistic gain during study abroad. *Foreign Language Annals, 40*(1): 43-61. https://doi:10.1111/j.1944-9720.2007.tb02853.x.

McGinn, G. (2015). *Foreign language, cultural diplomacy, and global security*. Cambridge, MA: American Academy of Arts and Sciences. Retrieved from https://amacad.org/multimedia/pdfs/Foreign-language-Cultural-Diplomacy-Global-Security.pdf.

Moyer, A. (2018). An advantage for age? Self-concept and self-regulation as teachable foundations in second language accent. *CATESOL Journal 30*(1): 95-112. https://doi.org/10.1080/17501229.2013.836205

Nishino, T., & Atkinson, D. (2015). Second language writing as sociocognitive alignment. *Journal of Second Language Writing 27*: 37-54.

Rifkin, B. (2005). A ceiling effect in traditional classroom foreign language instruction: Data from Russian. *Modern Language Journal, 89*(1): 3-18. https://doi.org/10.1111/j.0026-7902.2005.00262.x.

Rivers, W. P., & Brecht, R. D. (2018). America's languages: The future of language advocacy. *Foreign Language Annals, 51*(1), 24-34. https://doi:10.1111/flan.12320.

Roshandel, J., Ghonsooly, B., & Ghanizadeh, A. (2018). L2 motivational self-system and self-efficacy: A quantitative survey-based study. *International Journal of Instruction, 11*(1): 329-344. https://doi.org/10.12973/iji.2018.11123a.

Strid, J. E. (2017). The myth of the Critical Period. *TESOL Journal, 8*(3): 700-715. https://doi.org/10.1002/tesj.296.

Swender, E. (2003). Oral proficiency testing in the real world: Answers to frequently asked questions. *Foreign Language Annals, 36*(4): 520-526. https://doi.org/ 10.1111/j.1944- 9720.2003.tb02141.x.

Toner, M. (2019). Bringing study abroad home. *International Educator, 28*(1): 24-29.

Vanhove, J. (2013). The critical period hypothesis in second language acquisition: A statistical critique and a reanalysis. *PLoS ONE, 8*(7): 1-15. https://doi.org/10.1371/journal.pone.0069172.

Van Lier, L. (2000). From input to affordance: Socio-interactive learning from an ecological perspective. In J. Lantolf (Ed.), *Sociocultural theory and second language learning* (pp. 245-259). Oxford, UK: Oxford University Press.

Yin, R. K. (2018). *Case study research: Design and methods*. Thousand Oaks, CA: Sage.

About the Author

Dr. Jack Franke is Professor of Russian at the Defense Language Institute. He has authored or contributed several titles in the Department of Defense. He is the author of *The Big Silver Book of Russian Verbs* and *Streetwise Russian* with Audio CD: *Speak and Understand Everyday Russian*.

NOTE: The opinions in this article are those of the author alone and do not reflect the policies or opinions of the U.S. Defense Language Institute Foreign Language Center.

On the Cusp:
Zone of Proximal Development Tables to Guide Formative Assessment[6]

Betty Lou Leaver, MSI Press LLC (USA)

Abstract

The chasm between the successive proficiency levels (ILR 1, 2, 3, 4/ACTFL Novice, Intermediate, Advanced, Distinguished) is large. The Cusp Tables, developed with the support of the National Foreign Language Center, with input from large numbers of Level-4 language users and informed by proficiency testing instruments in use at the time, articulate proficiency elements believed to be most critical for passing from one level to the next. They suggest how to use this knowledge, along with formative assessment, to determine best next steps for individual learners based on their zones of proximal development (Vygotsky). The tables provided in this article for English, Russian, and Heritage Spanish can be used to guide the development of similar tables for other languages.

Keywords: proficiency cusps, cusp tables, zone of proximal development, formative assessment, proficiency levels

At the turn of this century, the "flights of fancy" of more progressive members of the profession were balanced out in nearly equal measure by the "stick-in-the-mud" preservationists. Change occurs incrementally and concurrently with changes in its environment—the politics of the day, extant educational philosophies, and the passing of the generations. What is defined as standard fare for learners advances slowly toward what is enthusiastically suggested and away from what is steadfastly offered, toward a focus on possibility (or, as its risk-taking proponents would insist, a new, adjusted reality)

---

6. The cusp tables (sometimes called grids during the early years of their evolution) described in this article were researched and designed together with the late Dr. Madeline Ehrman, administrator of foreign language education programs and research at the Foreign Service Institute and Associate at the National Foreign Language Center.

and away from an historically believed reality, and, as current progressive thinking would have it, toward increasing individualization and away from standardization.

Progress toward Near-Native Outcomes

It should be no surprise, then, that that 20-some years after the original theoretical work and research on what it takes to reach near-native levels of world language proficiency the supporting curricula and materials are still in the rarely existing and generally experimental state. Yet, we have made progress. We do indeed know more about how learners succeed and fail and how, in particular, near-native speakers (readers, listeners, writers) have acquired their proficiency, including the immensely differing paths taken by individuals (Franke, this volume; Mueller, 2003) and even by the same individual acquiring proficiency in multiple languages (Leaver & Atwell, 2002), and what is shared among all of them (see Bernhardt, this volume). As open architecture curriculum design (Leaver & Campbell, 2020), and testing and assessment have become better defined, especially formative assessment (e.g., diagnostic assessment; Cohen 2003, 2020; Corin & Entis, this volume; Dababneh & Yuan, forthcoming). And, as part of a special project supported by the National Foreign Language Center (NFLC), research was carried out with language-specific (Arabic, Russian, Spanish, Heritage Spanish) focus groups of learners, proficiency testers, and diagnostic assessors to determine the defining moments of when near-native was achieved—just what linguistic competencies and learning activities helped learners leap over the cusp from 3+ to 4, in the opinions of learners who had made that leap and those who had tested them.[7]

This article describes the origin, purpose, and application of the upper-level cusp tables for reading and listening generically and for Heritage Spanish specifically, as an example.[8] This article re-constructs, in part, the earlier (late 1990s) work of Ehrman and Leaver, using representative upper-level-proficiency tables that have survived the intervening years and have been used as formative assessment tools by individual teachers and testers in some programs at the Foreign Service Institute (FSI) and the Defense Language Institute Foreign Language Center (DLIFLC). The goal is to make the tables and the reasoning that underlies them available to other researchers, course designers, and language educators. While cusp tables do exist for lower levels, and in greater quantity, for the most part, they are less pertinent to the development of near-native proficiency.[9]

The CUSP Tables

---

7. This research informed the work of Ehrman and Leaver in drawing up the cusp tables. The original research included all levels from beginner to near-native, but for the purposes of this article, the focus is on the 3+/4 cusp. Indeed, within the NFLC project, the focus was preferentially on the high-end learner. Unfortunately, almost none of the research itself was ever published and exists today mainly in left-behind notes and the cusp tables themselves.

8. In the 1990s, a manual was developed by Ehrman and Leaver to accompany the tables; unfortunately, that manual appears to have been lost over time.

9. Cusp tables for all levels (such as have remained in existence into 2023) can be found at www.msipress.com/JDLS.

Definition of Cusp

If one considers a 3+ to be just a little less than a 4 (the "fallen angel" concept of "plus" levels, as opposed to the "rising star" concept which views 3+ as meaning merely "beyond the half-way point between 3 and 4"), the question becomes, "So, what is missing?" The "cusp" is the remaining area in front of Level 4 where something is (or some things are) missing. The missing piece could be a grammatical feature not yet under full control or an impoverished lexicon. It could be the nonnative-like use of expressions or collocations translated from English or cultural misunderstandings. It could be nonnative pronunciation. It could be all of the above or other phenomena that marks one as not yet almost native. A gray concept, to be sure. However, work with focus groups showed a fair amount of consensus in the identification of most of these "missing" phenomena; they are often, but not always, targets of assessment during oral proficiency interviews. The bottom line is that the cusp is a level of proficiency that is not quite at the next level but that exhibits most of the identifiers of the next level.

Identification of Cusps within Tabular Formats

The content within any cusp would have to be identified on a granular level in order to "push" a learner over the cusp; a generic description provides too little information to promote a helpful learning focus. For example, the ILR 4 speaking description says, in part, "Organizes discourse well, using appropriate rhetorical speech devices, native cultural references and understanding." How does a learner acquire appropriate rhetorical devices or native cultural references? What are those rhetorical devices? Are they the same across languages? Although they are clearly not, within a language family there would be some shared rhetorical devices. What are the cultural references? Do they come from literature? Social media? Children's games? Tribal customs? A generic description, as is given in the ILR proficiency level descriptions (or in the ACTFL proficiency descriptions), provides few hooks for a learning plan or approach.

The focus groups "sliced and diced" the content of the ILR proficiency descriptions for the upper levels of proficiency in particular, laying out a global proficiency "grid" (which morphed into tables) of 10 components of proficiency underlying their experiences in language acquisition to the near-native level. These components coincide to a great extent with the kinds of communicative competence components suggested by Mitrofanova (1996); they are identified below and in Appendices C and D.

In addition, reaching the granularity needed for any learner's language of study would require the incorporation of the uniqueness of that language, which, based upon input from the focus groups mentioned earlier, expands as one climbs higher up the proficiency scale, as well as a breakdown of those unique features into learnable units i.e., the identification of the rhetorical devices, cultural references, and much more. This would require another kind of table—specific language proficiency reflecting the unique features of a given language (under the umbrella of the GLP grid/table). In this two-step approach, the level descriptions could move from pure descriptions to learning content for a particular language, providing learner and teacher with a mechanism for preparing learning activities and measuring incremental progress across and over the cusp and into the next level.

Composing the Tables

Given this approach, two types of tables were composed. The first set were global language profile (GLP) tables that described the expected behaviors at each level of proficiency generic to the proficiency descriptions of the ILR, informed by the granularity proposed by the focus groups. (See Appendices A & B for examples.) The second set were language-specific and focused on the unique characteristics of a given language. (See Appendices C& D for examples.)

Keep in mind that the interest here was not the description of a proficiency level but rather the identification of individual language and cultural features within those levels that would define a "cusp" to be leapt over in passing from ILR 3+ to ILR 4. Initially, the lists of these very specific phenomena critical for leaping over the cusp of 3+ and into Level 4 were gathered into a set of 2-column GLP tables entitled. For a Level 4 to be achieved, all cusp items needed to be under control.

As mentioned above, to use the GLP tables to show specifically what might be missing was not possible because each language, it was found, had peculiarities that differed significantly from other languages. For example, aspect in Spanish is relatively straightforward in that it is essentially morphological with few irregularities and semantic consistency across verbal categories; hence, it could be expected to be mastered at earlier levels of proficiency. Aspect in Russian, however, is both morphologically and semantically complex and involves numerous subcategories (including semantic subcategories that vary based on situational use, the availability of multiple forms with semantic nuances in some cases (e.g., secondary imperfectives), differing use among verb classes, and greater complexities of formation and usage than in Romance languages, such as Spanish. Rarely have learners at levels lower than 4 actually mastered Russian aspect. (This particular example is discussed in greater detail below in the section on identifying ZPD.) On the other hand, the formation of the conditional mood is complex in Spanish and takes time to acquire; in Russian, the conditional can be taught at very early levels of proficiency since it is a combination of the particle *бы* with the past tense form, which itself is a structurally simple form for most, though not all, verbs. For this reason, GLP tables turned out to be insufficient, and an aforementioned second set of tables specifying language-specific features i.e., language specific profile (LSP) tables, was developed.

These LSP tables identified not only the behavior/specific skill expected at Level 4 but also what was typical at Level 3+. Thus, the missing language variables needed to move from 3+ to 4 were made clear so that they could be incorporated into instruction or learning plans.[10] The language-specific tables were drawn up to show what could be lacking in any individual at the 3+ level: the obstacle to that individual achieving Level 4 (column 2) aligned with what would be expected at Level 4 (column 3). Column 1

---

10. This was also the case with other levels: 0+1, 1+/2, and 2+/3. Although some of those tables do exist, they are not included here as they are only indirectly relevant to high-level language proficiency.

simply identifies the category of phenomena researched: general proficiency, strategic competence, sociocultural competence, fluency, and attentional focus.

GLP Tables

Unfortunately, while data were collected and tables composed for all four skill areas, those for the productive skills of writing and speaking have not been preserved in a comprehensive and currently available form.[11] For reading, the Defense Language Proficiency Test (DLPT) and the FSI reading tests were used, extrapolating what was common between them.[12] For listening, the DLPT was used. (FSI calculates the listening score from the OPI.) As noted earlier, added to the commonalities from the tests were commonly shared insights from the focus groups and discussions with individual high-level learners, all of whom had taken proficiency tests that showed them to be at Level 3+ or at Level 4 on the Interagency Language Roundtable (ILR) Skill Level Description scale (ILR, 2023).

At the higher levels of proficiency, the list of expected behaviors for the GLP tables (and for each of the other levels) can be quite long. The need to point out specific behaviors that are necessary to be acquired in order to cross from the 3+ level to Level 4.

The generic proficiency subscale of the GLP emphasizes the completeness of understanding and the recognition of lack of understanding subtleties. (In speaking, this subscale would include the ability of a speaker to draw out definitions and explanations without a native speaker listener becoming uncomfortable or even aware of the lack of understanding while the speaker filled in gaps quickly through natural elicitation techniques.) It also focused on reading fluency (approaching the speed of a native reader), reading/listening between the lines (what the author/speaker wanted the reader/listener to infer from the text), and reading beyond the lines (in what socio-political environment the text was written/delivered and how that colored the meaning, or what assumptions were made but not stated). The behaviors expected also included an understanding of style, understanding the difference between the written and spoken languages, and knowing who the author's target audience would be (and noticing how the author oriented his/her writing to the audience, thereby being able to interpret beyond the words correctly). In speaking, recognition and understanding of dialectal forms was important. In listening, there is the additional need to be able to understand language that is garbled, spoken in a noise environment, or distorted in some way.[13] Parallels in reading may be less common but can involve corrupted texts (such as often occurs in transcriptions of spoken text from

---

11. Efforts are currently underway to find and convert data recorded on software programs not readable by current computers. The possibility of recovering the writing and speaking tables from these older programs, as well as tables for other languages, remains promising.

12. The OPI formats differ between DLI and FSI, but the results are, arguably, very similar although Leaver and Atwell (2002) posit some important differences in the results and the reasons for them, with the FSI OPI allowing compensatory scoring and the DLIFLC OPI reflecting non-compensatory scoring. The ACTFL OPI was not used since all students/language users in the focus groups were US government employees.

13. At the DLIFLC, this kind of speech is referred to as "super-authentic."

meetings), incorrectly copied texts, incorrect or incomplete optical character recognition, or damaged or partially obscured text documents (for example, poorly photocopied texts, or a newspaper that has rubbed out words from too much handling—a problem that is quickly disappearing in the computer age), or extreme idiolectal use of the language. See Appendix A for a more complete listing of behaviors comprising the GLP associated with reading and Appendix B for those associated with listening.

Strategic Competence[14]

The strategic competence subscale of the GLP refers to the ways, means, and techniques (i.e., strategies) needed to process a text accurately. They include the range of language learning strategies (Oxford, 2017) employed at lower levels of proficiency as well as strategies specific to higher levels of text processing in any language as well as some specific to particular languages. The latter (those needed at higher proficiency levels) include advance preparation through research into the topic of the text. Among the former are using textual cues, filling in gaps through contextual cues, linguistic parsing, or knowledge of the bigger picture (who the author/speaker is, what s/he focuses on or what is his/her political leaning, and what texts have preceded the current one). See Appendix A for a more complete listing of behaviors comprising the strategic competence subscale associated with reading and Appendix B for those associated with listening.

Structural Competence

At Level 4, one expects to find complete understanding of grammatical and suprasegmental structures, including regional and social-class dialectal structure, which can differ considerably from the standard language. Often, dialects exhibit simplification of structure or syncretism of case forms. The underlying case is there; the distinction in form is not. So, the reader/listener is left to determine whether the lexical item being used has a dative, genitive, or prepositional case meaning, which is essential to understanding the meaning of a sentence, since in case languages, the case specifies the syntactic relation among words. At this proficiency level, archaic and substandard forms are also understood and processed as such. Further, Level 4 language learners are rarely confused by typographical error or mistakes in speaking (which all native speakers in all languages make upon occasion). See Appendix A for a more complete listing of behaviors comprising the structural competence subscale associated with reading and Appendix B for those associated with listening.

---

14. All the GLP subscales at Level 4 as listed in this article beg the question as to where Level 4 (native-like) ends and Level 5 (well educated native speaker) takes over. That question, while important, was not addressed by the focus groups whose task was to more specifically delineate Level 4 and what separates Level 4 from Level 3+.

Lexical Competence

Lexical competence focuses on the understanding of how words work in the particular language to the point that nonsense words are perceived in the same ways that native speakers perceive them, made-up words (for fun or for reason of purposeful idiosyncratic description) are realized for what they are and do not confuse the reader/listener, and obscure and non-standard lexemes, as well as jargon and dialectal vocabulary and neologisms, are either already a part of the learner's personal dictionary or are quickly understood and internalized. Listeners and readers at this level understand and enjoy word play. They also understand pretentious words that do not quite get to the point and those words that beginners often want to know but do not and cannot use appropriately: obscenities. At this level, learners prefer to use specialized dictionaries, as well as monolingual dictionaries. See Appendix A for a more complete listing of behaviors comprising the lexical competence subscale associated with reading and Appendix B for those associated with listening.

Discourse Competence

The discourse competence subscale assumes the understanding of most forms of discourse, including persuasion, counseling, negotiation, conjecture, editorials, debates, argumentation, and literary spoofs that would be considered accessible to the average educated native speaker. Level 4 language learners are also able to follow unpredicted turns in thought and recognize rhetorical devices, cohesive devices, and transitions, as well as rhetorical and archaic styles. They correctly interpret tone, sarcasm, irony, parody, metaphor, and intentional circumlocution and understand poorly structured and highly colloquial discourse. Further, they recognize poor discourse as well as erudite discourse and, in written skills, could proofread the work of native speakers. See Appendix A for a more complete listing of behaviors comprising the discourse competence subscale associated with reading and Appendix B for those associated with listening.

Sociolinguistic Competence

Level 4 language users recognize a wide range of registers: social, country vs city, dialectal, age, gender, class, professional, and more. They have knowledge of a wide range of acronyms, and they know the proper way to address superiors, colleagues, pets, strangers, and others. See Appendix A for a more complete listing of behaviors comprising the sociolinguistic competence subscale associated with reading and Appendix B for those associated with listening.

Sociocultural Competence

Level 4 assumes the ability to understand a wide range of literary allusions, culturally loaded expressions, and a wide range of historical, social, and folkloric references. Awareness of the times and understanding contemporary cultural artifacts are critical skill sets at this level. Also, learners at this level can appropriately interpret expressions of power, solidarity, and social rank. Here, in the realm of sociocultural competence, is where knowing how to play children's games becomes significant and quickly separates the non-native from the native. See Appendix A for a more complete listing of behaviors comprising the sociocultural competence subscale associated with reading and Appendix B for those associated with listening.

Emotional Competence

Emotional competence, a language feature first described by Eshkembeeva, (1997), encompasses the ability to correctly interpret emotional undertones of a text or "get" a literary character. Moreover, Level 4 language users understand emotions and emotional attributes in the way they are intended and interpreted in the native culture, not as they might be interpreted in the learner's culture. See Appendix A for a more complete listing of behaviors comprising the emotional competence subscale associated with reading and Appendix B for those associated with listening.

Fluency

Fluency here refers to the ease of processing written and oral texts. A characteristic that contributes to this is the ability to hold new words, expressions, grammatical forms, and cultural and sociolinguistic information in memory while processing known information in order to absorb it from context or redundancy.[15] They recognize that they have misread and take action to correct that. See Appendix A for a more complete listing of behaviors comprising the fluency subscale associated with reading and Appendix B for those associated with listening.

Attentional Focus

Attentional focus refers to what the reader or listener focuses on. At Level 4, according to research conducted on high-level students at the FSI (Leaver, 1986), learners focus on 1) unknown words, holding them in memory until they figure them out from context, fascinated by them, much as a native speakers would be; and 2) the same grammatical features that a native speaker would orient toward in processing meaning (e.g., syntax in English, case in Russian). See Appendix A for a more complete listing of behaviors comprising the attentional focus subscale associated with reading and Appendix B for those associated with listening.

---

15. In a survey conducted by Leaver (1986), learners who had reached Level 4 reported focusing on unknown words while reading and listening rather than on global meaning, as reported by learners at Level 3. Since this looked like exactly the same behavior reported by beginning learners, a follow-up survey was conducted to determine what, if any, difference there might be. The difference was great. The beginning learners were stopped by unknown words; those words caused confusion and subsequent disruption in thought, resulting in the inability to process the meaning of the text. The Level 4 learners had no difficulty processing the text and understanding the meaning of it; they were simply fascinated by new words and would hang onto them until the context allowed them to define and internalize them. They were, in essence, multi-tasking, which they could do because of their advanced knowledge of the language. The beginners were unable to multi-task and simply stopped reading or listening.

Using the Tables

Tables were prepared for a number of languages and were used by a subset of instructors at both the Foreign Service Institute and the Defense Language Institute Foreign Language Center. The tables are very detailed and, hence, large. Most programs that have used the cusp tables have printed them out onto letter-size, A4, or legal-size paper and laminated them as large cards, making them easier to manage.

As noted, not all of the tables have survived the intervening years. The ones most intact are those for Arabic, English, Russian, Spanish, and Heritage Spanish. Of these, only English and Heritage Spanish have survived for Level 4 cusp information (and, hence, included in the appendices for this article). However, an astute teacher and accomplished tester could use these two sets of tables to develop tables in other languages. The confidence in suggesting this is that the one constant among all the NFLC focus groups was the delineation of the ten subcategories comprising general proficiency.

The GLP Tables.

Appendix A contains the GLP table for reading: GLP 3+/4 Reading. Appendix B contains the generic table for listening: GLP 3+/4 Listening. These tables served as the resource for building the language-specific tables and were not used independently for purposes of formative assessment. While they begin with and are informed by the ILR skill level descriptions, those categories are too broad, too vague, and too generalized for diagnostic use. Languages differ in their features, a fact that is not reflected either in the ILR skill level descriptions nor in the more substantively delineated generic cusp tables. This reality prompted the development of LSP tables.

The LSP Tables

Appendix C and Appendix D provide samples of language-specific proficiency (LSP) tables.[16] For each cusp level of a given language, 10 LSP tables were developed, one for each of the subscales, based on the GLP tables. The LSP tables differed from the GLP tables in that the GLP tables were mainly descriptive whereas the LSP tables were intended for use both for ZPD identification and as goal-oriented teaching tools.

The three columns in the LSP tables identify the language feature of the subscale, current status (what the 3+ learner is able to do), and the goal (what the Level 4 learner will need to be able to do). The middle column, then, identifies ways in which a 3+ learner may be failing to cross over the line to Level 4 and serves as a rich source of information for determining the learner's *zone of proximal development* (ZPD) (Vygotsky 1934/1978) and the likely most beneficial learning activities/learning plans. In diagnostic assessment sessions, assessors can use these tables to identify a learner's progress: where the learner is exhibiting a typical 3+ current status and where the learner is exhibiting already mastered

---

16. The large number of LSPs needed for just one cusp level across reading, writing, listening and speaking skills (a total of 40 tables) prohibits including more than a sample here. Others can be found at www.msipress.com/jdls/.

Level 4 behavior. The fewer Level 3+ behaviors, the closer the learner is to getting over the cusp; activities aimed at pushing the learner from the 3+ behavior to the 4 behaviors for particular language features can help speed up the process of achieving near-native proficiency. Most important, these tables provide a substantive basis for developing individualized learning plans for each learner and individualization of curricula to meet the specific needs of groups of learners.

Discussion

This discussion focuses on the language-specific tables since the GLP tables simply establish the background against which the LSP tables were developed. Specifically, this discussion will refer to aspects of Russian, Spanish, and Heritage Spanish since these are the only fully complete tables that remain.

Significance of the Subscales

The significance of each of the ten subscales has been described above in providing the definition of each. Of note is the fact that subscales do not necessarily line up with OPI subscales; there was a need, in determining ZPD, to break the overall scale down more finitely. One of the models used to identify appropriate subdivisions was the description of communicative competence (and the testing of proficiency as communicative competence) by Mitrofanova (1996). Other breakdowns came through shared consensus of focal groups of Level 4 language professionals, convened by the NFLC in the years 2000-2003. Yet others came from a qualitative study of over 100 Level 4 language users, guided by the DLIFLC and supported by the NFLC (Leaver & Atwell, 2002)

From Generic to Specific

Typically, proficiency tests, such as those administered by the DLIFLC, the FSI, and the American Council on the Teaching of Foreign Languages, are by nature and intent highly generalizable. The proficiency descriptions can be used for any and all languages. This allows for very broad descriptions of each proficiency level, so broad that it is not possible to teach to the next level of proficiency with any kind of precision or individualization because the level is not precisely defined and the intent is global, not general, grading (i.e., level identification).

The master set of generic tables was not meant to be used in formative/diagnostic assessment but rather to serve as a guide in the development of the language-specific tables. They did not contain the specificity necessary for application to proficiency improvement. The LSP cusp tables, which broke down in detail the language features for each given language needed at each base level (e.g., Level 4) and present at the cusp level (Level 3+), provided both a testing tool for determining whether a learner, for any given language feature, was functioning receptively and productively at the target base proficiency level (here, Level 4) or at the cusp level (here, Level 3+). Based on those assessments, it became possible for those testers and teachers using the tables to determine how to help learners move over the cusp into the target base level.

Determining ZPD

To move learners quickly up the proficiency ladder, it helps to know exactly what they are ready to learn next—the specific components of the next-higher level of proficiency, not the general description of the level. The most effective means of increasing a learner's proficiency rapidly is to orient instruction and learning materials toward the learner's ZPD, the space between what a learner can do on his/her own and what a learner can do with assistance. Using the cusp tables in testing (typically, formative assessment) allows a tester or teacher to determine, for example, which features of aspect have been acquired as exhibited by appropriate usage, which are in the process of being acquired as exhibited by both correct and incorrect usage, and which are not part of the learner's conversational/comprehension repertoire. Learners will exhibit language that has already been acquired, language that has been partially acquired, and language that is still being learned or still waiting to be learned.[17] It is the partially acquired language that falls in the learner's ZPD. As learners turn partially acquired language features into fully acquired ones, their ZPD moves to the ones that they were initially learning but that now are likely partially acquired through incidental, rather than intentional, exposure—and the work now becomes intentional.

For example, control of aspect is important for Level 4 proficiency in Slavic languages, but aspect is a complex category that includes multiple semantic, syntactic, and morphological elements. A learner might already be able to handle aspect that is determined by verbs that exhibit telicity but not for atelic verbs or verbs that have secondary imperfectives, are unpaired, have differing lexical bases for perfective and imperfective forms, have choices of multiple prefixes (with differing meaning) for perfective forms, verbs of motion, cases in which negative modality is present, or specific verbs in which the lexical component takes precedence over the grammatical component in determining aspectual use, among many more considerations. Simply determining that learners have not fully acquired aspect is not enough. Which verbs are controlled and which are not? What kinds of perfective and imperfective situations are understood and which are not? Expecting learners to uniformly develop an understanding of aspect and the ability to apply it routinely as a general category with multiple features (or subcategories) slows the pace to overall acquisition of aspect; add to that all the rich variation among verbs in how aspect is realized, and it is no wonder that it can take many, many years for learners of Russian to acquire aspect. The key is to determine which categories of verbs are starting to make sense to, and are coming under control for, the learner through skillful diagnostic testing, which, unlike summative proficiency tests that seek to establish a level, allows the tester to provide hints and help to the learner to determine where a little help results in success; where a little help produces success is the sweet spot, the ZPD.

Deluging the learner with categories of aspect already acquired does not represent the best use of classroom (or homework) time. Deluging learners with verbs that are still

---

17. Here the dichotomy suggested by Krashen (1982) is being used. While the underlying theory of this dichotomy has limitations and has upon many occasions been met with skepticism and questions, it serves a useful and pragmatic purpose for application of the cusp tables.

out of reach ensures mostly frustration and limited acquisition. Immersing learners in those that the learner can manage to use with a little help moves the learning along faster because the learner is ready to acquire these features.

ZPD is individual. All of the learners within a course will not acquire language features in the same order; much the way that vocabulary is acquired is based on personal situational need, and the same is true of grammatical features. This difference is so great between second-language learners and heritage learners that different cusp tables were made for each group of learners. In the aforementioned case of aspect, for example, heritage learners often exhibit tense-aspect restructuring (perhaps the influence of the dominant language in the community in which they live), such that aspect remains constant for telic verbs but is replaced by tense for atelic verbs (Laleko, 2009). Even where heritage and non-heritage learners are segregated, learners learn differently and acquire language features at different times. Hence, any program using diagnostic assessment and the cusp tables will yield highly individualized instruction and lessons.

Individualized Learning Plans

Some of the programs using the cusp tables prepared individualized learning plans (ISPs) for enrolled learners (Leaver, 2003). These could take short-term forms for learners in a classroom in an intensive environment, in which goals were quickly achieved, due in part to increased time on task or longer-term, even year-long ISPs, for learners working independently with a tutor outside of a formal program. (In the case of the latter, typically, a formative assessment was completed to determine each learner's ZPD, the results of which, combined with each learner's goals, were coalesced into an ISP prepared through discussion and negotiation with the individual learner.)

Conclusion

The primary purpose of this article is to share the concept of "cusp" in moving from one proficiency level to another as an aspect of the individual nature of language acquisition, as well as to document the history of the concept to the greatest extent possible. An important part of this purpose is to preserve those GLP and LSP tables that exist today in an effort to make them available to other researchers, testers, and teachers—and others—not only for use as is but also as models for reconstructing the missing tables as well as moving on to other languages beyond the four (Arabic, Russian, Spanish, and Heritage Spanish) originally produced as part of the NFLC project described here.

The tables at hand have been used continuously from 2006-2023 at the DLIFLC, where diagnostic assessors have found them especially helpful. They have also been used by DLIFLC intermediate/advanced[18] course instructors as a way to gather and provide targeted feedback to learners about their language development and needs. It is the author's

---

18. The DLIFLC course names do not align with ACTFL proficiency levels. At DLIFLC, intermediate courses have a graduation requirement of 2+; many of them in the 2006-2017 period of time saw outcomes of Levels 3, 3+, and 4. Similarly, the advanced courses had a graduation requirement of Level 3; many of them saw outcomes of 3+ and 4.

hope that others will adopt the concepts, use the tables, and build upon them. This could be done via a grant for a project that emulates the NFLC project that produced the table. Perhaps by a working group of interested researchers, testers, teachers, and other experts/users experienced at all levels of instruction (including Level 4) could pull together the needed focus groups. It could also be a challenging dissertation topic for graduate students who could do the research, gain access to high-level learners, and develop the LSP tables for their own specialty language.

While the partial set of tables in use at government language programs have been found to be helpful, a complete set would become a valuable resource in any proficiency-oriented program, especially those with specific outcome objectives, and for any individual learner at any level of proficiency—but particularly at the higher levels where so few resources exist—desirous and capable of developing his/her own accelerated learning program.[19]

References

Cohen, B. (2003). *Diagnostic assessment at the 3+/4 threshold*. Salinas, CA: MSI Press.

Cohen, B. (2020). *Diagnostic assessment at the 3+/4 threshold*. Hollister, CA: MSI Press. (second, expanded edition)

Dababneh, R., & R. Yuan. (forthcoming) Open architecture curricular design as an enabler of diagnostic instruction. In A. Corin, C. Campbell, & B. L. Leaver (eds.), *Open architecture curriculum design*. Washington, DC: Georgetown University Press.

Eshkembeeva, L. V. (1997). Emotional competence. Paper presented at MAPRIAL (International Association of Teachers of Russian Language and Literature) International Congress, Moscow.

Interagency Language Roundtable. (2023). *Proficiency level descriptions*. Downloaded from www.govtilr.org.

Krashen, S. D. 1982. *Principles and practice in second language acquisition*. Oxford, UK: Pergamon.

Laleko, O. 2009. *On covert tense-aspect restructuring in heritage Russian: A case of aspectually transient predicates*. Somerville, MA: Cascadilla Press.

Leaver, B. L. 1986. Hemisphericity of the brain and foreign language teaching. Benjamin Stolz, ed., *Folia Slavica* 8(1): 76-90.

Leaver, B. L. (2003). *Individualized learning plans for very advanced students of foreign languages*. Salinas, CA: MSI Press.

---

19. Acknowledgements are made to the following individuals without whose efforts this article could not have been written: Andrew Corin (who provided essential feedback to concepts and explications and urged the writing and publication of this article to ensure that the disappearing cusp information would remain available to those who can make good use of it), Madeline Ehrman (who, together with the author, conducted the research and formulated the tables), Sergey Entis (who applied the tables and maintained the tables through years of dormancy), the NFLC (which funded the bulk of the research, especially the focus groups), the U.S. Department of State's Foreign Service Institute (FSI) (which supported Ehrman's continuation of the NFLC project through interviewing high-level language users as well as proficiency testers and diagnostic assessors at the FSI), and the countless language learners/users and DA and OPI testers who readily shared their insights from conducting dozens and, in some cases, hundreds of high-level language tests.

Leaver, B. L., & Atwell, S. (2002). In B. L. Leaver & B. S. Shekhtman (eds.), *Developing professional-level foreign language proficiency*. Cambridge, UK: Cambridge University Press.

Leaver, B. L., & Campbell. C. (2020). *The art of teaching Russian*. Washington, DC: Georgetown University Press.

Mitrofanova, Olga Danilovna, ed. 1996. *Threshold Level: Russian Language: Volume 1: Everyday Communication* (title translated from Russian). Moscow: Sovet Evropy Press.

Mueller, C. 2003. Tracing the steps of the successful multilingual: A synopsis. *Journal for Distinguished Language Studies* 1 (1): 51-58.

Oxford, R. L. (2017). *Teaching and researching language learning strategies: Self-regulation in context*. London: Routledge.

Vygotsky, L. (1934/1978). *Mind in society: The development of higher psychological processes*. Cambridge, MA: Harvard University Press.

About the Author

Betty Lou Leaver Ph.D., (Pushkin Institute, Moscow) is Managing Editor at MSI Press LLC and retired provost at the Defense Language Institute Foreign Language Center. She has also directed language programs at the Foreign Institute and NASA and served as consultant to language programs in 24 countries. She has published more than a dozen books on second language acquisition and specializes in higher levels of language proficiency.

APPENDIX A
Global Learning Profile for Level 4 Reading
GLP 3+/4 Reading

Category	*Expected Behaviors*
General Proficiency	understands all forms and styles of texts pertinent to professional, personal, and social needs that would be considered accessible to the average educated native speaker
	recognizes lack of comprehension
	understands subtleties, nuances, and cultural and literary allusions that would be considered accessible to the average educated native speaker
	understands language tailored to specific audiences that would be considered accessible to the average educated native speaker
	interpretations compare closely with those of college-educated native readers in dealing with the text
	understands significance of register or shifts in register that would be considered accessible to the average educated native speaker
	detects bias
	reads quickly
	exhibits stamina in reading copious amounts of authentic material and in reading for long periods of time
	understands code switching that can occur in the writings of immigrant speakers of the target language
	reads between the lines in accurately interpreting authorial intent
	accurately derives implicit meaning from the text
	interpretation compares closely with those of educated native speakers in dealing with the text
	recognizes intentional ambiguity

Strategic Competence	plans approach to reading an authentic text in advance, using logic and linguistic means available
	knows purpose and adjusts strategies accordingly
	uses resources appropriately, including reference materials
	recognizes the need for and makes course corrections
	identifies clues to understanding within a text, including ellipses
	adjusts reading approach to meet the demands of the text
	confirms and adjusts interpretation as reading progresses
	compares texts to genre models
	uses endurance strategies in reading long or many texts; paces self
	uses mapping strategies
	uses strategies of comparison and sophisticated forms of relationship
	self-corrects in presence of prediction and conjecture errors
	knows where to find working aids and uses them appropriately
	develops individual and automatic mechanisms to self-assess reading
	uses knowledge of scripts, narrative structure, grammatical competence, and lexical probabilities to understand intent where there is typographical error
	uses knowledge of scripts to fill in letters and words from lines that disappear when paper is folded or are missing for other reasons
	uses mental and other forms of outlining in reading
	uses sophisticated prediction strategies
	uses integration strategies
	uses networking strategies

Structural Competence	exhibits complete understanding of grammatical structure, including in many social and geographic dialects and many obscure, archaic, or, in languages where applicable, literary form
	recognizes the difference between formal and informal writing styles
	understands specifics of formal writing styles, including creative forms of structural use in writing, such as, in some languages, reflexification (e.g., conversion of a transitive verb into an impersonal reflexive for appropriate subtle meaning change) and syntax modification, is not confused by typographical errors
	follows language structure that is purposely manipulated for rhetorical effect
	understands substandard grammar
	comprehends subtle differences among synonymous structural expressions
	understands structures and grammatical rules in reading that differ from those used in speaking
	notices, but is not confused by, intentional grammatical deviations

Lexical Competence	understands a range of jargon from many areas, including professional disciplines, child language, "kitchen talk," colloquialisms, and street language
	understands with near-complete accuracy any standard and commonly used lexical item, as well as many obscure lexemes
	understands crude, obscene, and boorish language and its implications
	understands most word play
	understands artificial and idiosyncratic words, created for a specific purpose, when the context is known
	understands substandard lexicon
	understands pretentious language that does not get to the point
	understands the total lexical system (formation, derivation, etc.)
	recognizes stylistically appropriate and inappropriate use of lexicon
	recognizes genre-appropriate and genre-inappropriate use of lexicon
	understands word formation and the meaning of innovated words
	comprehends subtle differences among synonymous words and phrases
	understands a wide range of acronyms
	understands technical writing in fields of expertise
	appropriately employs a wide range of lexical tools: monolingual dictionaries, medical dictionaries, grammatical (orthographic) dictionaries, derivational dictionaries, special terminology dictionaries

Discourse Competence	understands most forms of discourse, including persuasion, counseling, negotiation, conjectural materials, editorials, and literary spoofs, that would be considered accessible to the average educated native speaker
	recognizes erudite forms of discourse structures as erudite and interprets them accurately
	correctly interprets tone: irony, sarcasm, intentional circumlocution
	recognizes stylistic errors
	correctly interprets most metaphors
	comprehends subtle differences among synonymous forms of discourse
	exhibits sensitivity to context and understands through contextualized meaning
	understands in many instances in spite of poorly written discourse, including substandard language, as well as inappropriate or missing discourse devices
	displays competence at text deconstruction
	has appropriate genre expectations
	understands when a text follows or deviates from expected narrative structure
	follows unpredictable turns in thought
	recognizes rhetorical organization and its implication for style and meaning
	in most cases, understands intended meaning in spite of missing cohesive devices
	recognizes transitions, understands texts that lack them or authors that use them poorly
	understands a comprehensive range of rhetorical styles
	understands many, if not most, archaic styles
	understands the significance of semiotic devices
Sociolinguistic Competence	recognizes and understands professional, social, dialectal, age, gender, and country versus city registers
	recognizes appropriateness of forms of address for elders, children, pets, strangers, professionals, and others
	correctly interprets slang as used by various social classes
	correctly interprets professional jargon
	understands a wide range of acronyms from a variety of common and specific fields

Sociocultural Competence	understands nearly all literary allusions in reading texts of all varieties (classical literature, popular literature, and interpersonal written communications) that would be considered accessible to the average educated native speaker
	reads beyond the lines, using knowledge of cultural and generational backgrounds for accurate interpretation
	understands culturally loaded expressions and prolepsis
	correctly interprets religious references
	correctly interprets historical references
	correctly interprets folkloric references
	correctly interprets references to children's literature, games, and songs
	understands most allusions in popular journals to popular culture artifacts
	nearly always responds appropriately to expressions of power, solidarity, and social rank shown in written communication as it is expressed in the target culture (via grammatical forms, particles, lexical choices, etc.)
Emotional Competence	understands personality attributes of the author based on the manner in which they are described or expressed in target-culture ways that differ from native culture
	understands emotional attributes built into the text (e.g., character intent in literary pieces)
Fluency	holds new words, expressions, grammatical forms, and cultural and sociolinguistic information in memory while processing known information in order to absorb it from context or redundancy
	is aware when misreading occurs and is able to modify interpretation
	structural and visual elements of text processing are normally automatic and secondary to communication
	handles most handwriting and nearly all types of fonts
Attentional Focus	directs attention to unknown words and phrases, which are found to be intriguing, and new ways of expressing ideas
	pays attention to the same elements of rhetoric as native speakers

APPENDIX B
GLP 3+/4 Listening

Category	Expected Behaviors
General Proficiency	understands all forms and styles of speech pertinent to professional, personal, and social needs, even in many unfavorable conditions (loudspeakers, static, etc.)
	understands subtleties, nuances, and cultural and literary allusions in standard and dialectal forms – and recognizes the regionalizations
	understands language tailored to specific audiences and the standard and non-standard formats and text organizations needed to accomplish tailoring
Strategic Competence	recognizes need for and makes course corrections
	fills in gaps through clues, including elliptical and non-cohesive speech
	uses advanced organization
Structural Competence	exhibits complete understanding of grammatical and suprasegmental structure, including in many dialects
	hears errors made by native speakers but is not confused by them
Lexical Competence	understands with near-complete accuracy any standard and commonly used lexical item, as well as many obscure lexemes
	understands jargon from many areas, including professional disciplines, child language, "kitchen talk," culturally loaded expressions, and street language
	understands word play
	understands some dialectal speech, including dialectal changes in morphology, syntax, intonation, pronunciation, and lexicon
Discourse Competence	understands all forms of discourse, including persuasion, counseling, negotiation, conjectural materials, editorials, and literary spoofs
	follows unpredictable turns in thought
	understands rhetorical organization
	recognizes cohesive devices, sign-posting, and transitions
	understands rhetorical style, including archaic styles

Sociolinguistic Competence	recognizes and understands professional, social, dialectal, age, gender, and country versus city registers, including jargon, slang, and commonly used ungrammatical language
	recognizes appropriateness of forms of address for elders, children, pets, strangers, professionals, and others
	Understands ellipses, filling in the unspoken words conceptually
	Understands intention where language is misspoken, garbled, incomplete, and otherwise not of literary standard
	Understands significance of intonational patterns and intentional stress
Sociocultural Competence	understands nearly all literary allusions in listening texts of all varieties (podcasts, broadcasts, conversations, overheard conversations, lectures) that would be considered accessible to the average educated native speaker
	understands beyond the words (what is not said), using knowledge of cultural and generational backgrounds for accurate interpretation
	understands culturally loaded expressions and prolepsis
	correctly interprets religious references
	correctly interprets historical references
	correctly interprets folkloric references
	correctly interprets references to children's literature, games, and songs
	understands most allusions to popular culture artifacts
	nearly always responds appropriately to expressions of power, solidarity, and social rank shown in oral communication as it is expressed in the target culture (via grammatical forms, particles, lexical choices, etc.)
Emotional Competence	understands personality attributes of speakers based on word choices and intonation expressed in target-culture ways that differ from native culture
	understands body language that accompanies visual spoken texts
Fluency	holds new words, expressions, grammatical forms, and cultural and sociolinguistic information in memory while processing known information in order to absorb it from context or redundancy
	is aware when misunderstanding occurs and is able to modify interpretation
	structural and auditory elements of oral text processing are normally automatic and secondary to comprehension, including garbled speech
	handles most variations in speed of speech from slow to rapid to perfunctory and pro-forma

Attentional Focus	directs attention to unknown words and phrases, which are found to be intriguing, and new ways of expressing ideas
	pays attention to the same elements of speech as native speakers: significance of intonation, meaningful use of pauses, implied meaning

APPENDIX C

Heritage Spanish, Lexical Competence, Reading 3+/4

Language Feature	Current Status	Objectives
LF 1: Key words for author's spin	Identifies 50-60% of key words that signal author's intent, but has difficulty establishing all possible meanings	Identifies with accuracy 80% + of key words that signal author's intent, and establishes multiple meanings (e.g., What does the author mean by *guerras ajenas* in the following context: *Un lector se soprende de que yo califique el narcotráfico y la violación de los derechos humanos como 'guerras ajenas'*; or, What are the possible interpretations of the word Haití in the following: *Al paso que vamos, Colombia mirare con envidia el desempeño de todas las clases dirigentes del continente, incluida la de Haití*)
LF 2: Complex and culturally loaded texts by using background information, contextual cues, and socio-linguistic factors	Has limited ability to decode culturally loaded texts and needs assistance in order to process socio-linguistic terms and/or context (e.g., *Madrazo* [a Mexican politician who died in an airplane accident] *se dio el último madrazo* [died])	Uses topical, experiential, cultural, and linguistic knowledge resources to decode culturally loaded text with precision and accuracy
LF 3: Rhetorical figures	Identifies rhetorical figures, but does not consistently interpret them accurately	Consistently extracts author's intent (use of nuances, subtleties, and other stylistic devices) through successful interpretation of rhetorical figures

APPENDIX D
Heritage Spanish, Sociocultural Competence, Reading 3+/4

Language Feature	Current Status	Objectives
LF 1: Cultural references	Comprehends many socio-linguistic and cultural references within own culture (e.g., *Algunos lo califican de dinosaurio al Comandante Castro*)	Understands almost all socio-linguistic and cultural references across cultures and relates them to real world knowledge (e.g., *Con la apertura de la simbólica Puerte de Brandemburgo, el marxismo-leninismo perdió su más importante batalla de la guerra fría...*)
LF 2: Socio-cultural content	Has broad socio-cultural knowledge of self-country, but limited knowledge of other Spanish speaking countries	Calls on broad socio-cultural knowledge of many Spanish-speaking countries to correctly interpret texts in job related areas (e.g., *Unos billetes, con la imagen del licenciado en Derecho José Cecilio del Valle, eran suficientes para acortar períodos de cinco años y reducirlos en unas cuantas horas que se consumían en ponerse de acuerdo con el precio del título, tomarse la fotografía y proceder a elaborar el cartón, y, desde luego, comprar el clavo en la ferretería para colgar en la pared el honroso reconocimiento de haber concluído un periodo de studio*)

LF 3: Decoding specific regionalisms by using highly contextualized and conceptualized cues and nuances	Misses or misuses some cues and nuances needed to interpret regionalisms accurately (e.g., *El neoliberalismo en la economia*; *El impacto del estadismo* [State-owned business] *en la industria*; *Las politicas nacionalistas*...)	Grasps the meaning of culturally-loaded regionalisms by carefully analyzing them from the perspective of the target language and culture, the author and intended audience (e.g., Interprets that in Spain, *políticas nacionalistas* refer to autonomous regions in Spain and not to the central government)

Protocol-Based Formative Assessment: Evolution and Revolution at the Defense Language Institute Foreign Language Center

Andrew R. Corin and Sergey Entis
Defense Language Institute Foreign Language Center (USA)

Abstract

Protocol-based formative assessment (PBFA) can be a powerful tool for enhancing learning and diagnosing learning challenges. Yet there is an inherent tension between effectiveness and efficiency in the delivery of PBFA. This can be addressed through a variety of strategies: "rationing" PBFA to instances of individual learning difficulties, applying PBFA to all students but in fewer instances, or by engineering greater efficiency into the protocol. Regardless of the strategy adopted, it is taken for granted that PBFA should be maximally integrated with instruction-based formative assessment (IBFA) as an integral component of day-to-day classroom instruction. This article articulates the dilemma as it developed at the Defense Language Institute Foreign Language Center (DLIFLC) between 1989 and 2015 and the path pursued to overcome it through re-design of PBFA.

Keywords: diagnostic assessment; formative assessment; dynamic assessment; zone of proximal development; learner variables; learning styles; text typology; language proficiency; world language education; foreign language learning; Defense Language Institute Foreign Language Center

This article examines the development of formative assessment processes at the Defense Language Institute Foreign Language Center (DLIFLC) in the period between

1989 and 2015 with a focus on *diagnostic assessment* (DA).[20] DA is a protocol-based formative (PBFA) mechanism and an integral component of the concept of diagnostic instruction at the core of DLIFLC instructional strategy. DA has become a valuable tool for the analysis of student learning difficulties, and a fundamental component of efforts to optimize performance of all students. While DA is also borrowed for purposes that may be considered summative, its primary use is as a component of the learning process—to articulate learners' individual characteristics and needs, streamline learning for each, and diagnose and address learning difficulties.

The goals of DA overlap with those of dynamic assessment (as articulated in Poehner, 2008), but are broader in the development and exploitation of "learner profiles" (Sections 2-3, below). In recent years, the attempt to identify and exploit learners' "zone of proximal development" (ZPD, as defined in sociocultural theory and applied also in dynamic testing; see Lantolf & Thorne, 2006; Poehner, 2008) has been incorporated into DA training, thus bringing the approaches closer together.

Section 2 provides an overview of the DLIFLC learning context. It describes features that distinguish DLIFLC from most educational institutions, making it a unique environment for intensive observation of the effects of particular instructional practices. Section 3 sketches the origins and early development of DA. Section 4 examines DA as practiced during the decade through 2015. Section 5 explores how DA protocol was incorporated into instructional practice and quality management during this period, while Section 6 examines DA training. Two paramount lessons emerge from these last two sections. The first, now taken for granted in much of the L2 instructional community, concerns IBFA. This is the understanding that instructors should be constantly attuned to the cognitive styles, strategies, and relevant life experience of each learner, as well as to their current profiles of strengths and weakness viewed dynamically, adjusting activities for both individuals and cohorts to meet current needs. The second lesson concerns inherent tensions between effectiveness and efficiency in PBFA. Simply stated, the time and effort required for effective application of PBFA can become burdensome, while the training and skill maintenance required for effective application can strain or exceed institutional capacity. These tensions can adversely affect PBFA effectiveness as well as instructor and student morale. Sections 7 and 8 outline efforts to overcome this dilemma, and thus achieve the benefits of diagnostic instruction maximally informed by both PBFA and IBFA.

---

20. This paper was drafted in 2015 and reflects circumstances at that time, during which the authors played leading roles in the development of DA processes and training, culminating in a DA revision project during the years 2014-2015. The insights gained from that project remain valuable today. The authors' leadership roles in DA development concluded following closure of DLIFLC's Diagnostic Assessment Center and reassignment of its tasks to DLIFLC's Language Science & Technology Directorate. They are grateful to Betty Lou Leaver, Steven Koppany, and Bella Cohen for the invaluable recollections they provided concerning the background and development of DA at DLIFLC.

Defense Language Institute Foreign Language Center

During the period in question, some 3,500 students were typically enrolled in DLIFLC's resident initial acquisition (basic) programs in more than two dozen languages, each with 6 or 7 contact hours daily, for between 6 and (more typically) 12 or 18 months. Numerous other students enhanced their proficiencies through DLIFLC's post-basic programs, which included both resident and technology-mediated courses delivered from DLIFLC's home location in Monterey, California. Both post-basic and basic programs were also delivered throughout the world by *language training detachments* stationed at various locations or by *mobile training teams* that would travel to required locations. Other languages with smaller programs were served from DLIFLC's Washington, D.C. office. The graduation objective for DLIFLC basic courses was ILR Level 2+ in listening and reading and Level 2 in speaking, while the graduation requirement was 2/2/1+ in the same skills, respectively. Post-basic courses sought to achieve *global language proficiency* (GLP) at or above ILR Level 3, with an increasing proportion of students exiting at ILR 3+ or 4 in one or more modality.

A key distinguishing feature of DLIFLC's learning environment is accountability for proficiency outcomes. Each student represents a large investment allocated to meet some service or agency requirement. Conversely, students' careers as language professionals depend upon achieving or exceeding GLP standards and other language-related learning objectives. Add to these factors the large number of students processed year-round and the real-world stakes that depend on graduates' abilities, and it becomes clear that DLIFLC must closely monitor the performance of each program and student, taking all possible measures to enhance performance. At course completion students take standardized proficiency tests: Defense Language Proficiency Test (DLPT) in reading and writing, and the Oral Proficiency Interview (OPI).

Yet high stakes and high-stakes exams do not ensure success. For this reason, formative assessment played an ever-increasing role in the DLIFLC learning process during this period, becoming integrated, in differing ways, into both basic and post-basic DLIFLC courses.

Development of Diagnostic Assessment (DA)

DA arose at DLIFLC out of the practice of providing formative feedback based on immediate recall protocol (in the sense of Bernhardt & James, 1987) and learning styles beginning around 1989. The term "diagnostic assessment" was applied later, in 1997-1998, when it was assessed that what was missing from formative assessment processes at DLIFLC was utilization of the ILR scale for formative purposes through a standards-based matrix, and foundations were laid for a DA protocol encompassing the modalities of listening, reading, and speaking.

The new protocol included a diagnostic interview by two native speaker interviewers, who would present authentic content and elicit a ratable and analyzable sample, somewhat in the manner of an oral proficiency interview. Selection of materials was governed by text typology (TT) in the sense arising out of Child (1987), which roughly means establishing the ILR level of any reading text based on criteria analogous to those used to establish the ILR level of a ratable speech sample. TT is a discrete skill requiring norming. DA interviewers would use a "package" of texts, each rated at a specific ILR level and each associated with a unique set of comprehension questions requiring proficiency at the specified level. Interviewers would adapt the interview up or down depending on the proficiencies demonstrated by the learner. Initially, assessment teams were formed for Russian, Spanish, Korean, Chinese, and Arabic, with Persian Farsi added in 2000. Two DA specialists were allotted per language. The developers were aware of the range of extra-linguistic individual variables (cognitive styles, etc.) relevant to L2 learning, but did not feel that it was feasible to encompass them within the initial DA protocol.

The goal of the DA interview was not merely to determine GLP levels and specific strengths and weakness; analogous to dynamic assessment, it sought to identify areas that learners needed to address in order to achieve the next level of GLP, focusing on those within their immediate grasp (not yet referred to at this point as ZDP).

Rating and analysis of elicited samples and development of individualized learning plans (LPs) was based on the ILR Level Descriptions for each skill.

Following its inception in 1998, DA was offered on an on-demand basis to DLIFLC schools and external clients; it was recommended to basic-program schools that they perform one DA for each student at the end of the second semester (of a three-semester program), in time to address lacunae and make adjustments. Some department chairs preferred to perform DA earlier, at the end of the first semester.

The fact that DA was based on the ILR scale (like the DLPT) stimulated popularity, and numerous clients came forth, some using DA for purposes (placement, syllabus design, materials selection, program validation, etc.) beyond its intended purpose of enhancing efficiency of the learning process through individualization of instruction.

The popularity of DA, however, soon led to resource issues that limited DLIFLC's ability to apply DA as broadly and effectively as planners envisioned. One major issue was the labor-intensiveness of the process. When performed according to specifications, each DA could require as much as 13 hours of effort. The initial two-person teams per language could not meet demand, and routine use of multiple iterations of DA within a course clearly could not yet be anticipated.

The labor-intensiveness of DA gave rise in 2002 to idea of online diagnostic assessment (ODA), since it was felt that face-to-face DA couldn't meet demand on a cost-effective basis. ODA for reading and listening is now available through the DLIFLC internet site for many languages, though face-to-face DA remains the preferred model when feasible, allowing for more articulated and individualized analysis and treatment.

Yet another deleterious effect arose out of efforts to cope with the labor-intensiveness of the process. In response to tedium and time pressure, a tendency arose for DA specialists to take short cuts, e.g., "templatizing" individual LPs, so that the crucially individual aspect of the LP was lost, devolving into generic statements. This difficulty was exacerbated by the limited ability of some DA specialists, native speakers of the target language, to compose feedback and recommendations in adequate English, especially as learning approached higher levels.

From the point of view of the teaching departments, allotting time for DA from an already tight program was inconvenient and could be evaluated as counter-productive if evidence of a positive effect on learning outcomes was not manifest. This became likely if DA was performed in a rushed, pro forma manner, leading to a vicious circle. The desire of departments to work DA into their programs in the most efficient manner led in some cases to an especially pernicious effect which undermined DA's entire premise: since evaluation of a learner's current GLP level was one aspect of DA, some departments began to use DA for summative purposes, e.g., in lieu of unit or end-of-semester tests. When this occurred, DA came to be perceived by students as a summative measure and was received by them with all the enthusiasm usually adhering to tests.

In 2000 the School of Continuing Education (SCE) was created to house DLIFLC's intermediate and advanced courses, distance learning, and a range of outreach programs, including DA. DA development and delivery proceeded for some two years before going dormant for lack of funding. One major advance during this period was the regular provision of DA in support of the Defense Threat Reduction Agency, whose interpreters are trained by DLIFLC.

During fiscal year 2006, program budget decision PBD 753 provided funding for eight DA specialists for the Directorate of Undergraduate Education (UGE, which encompassed DLIFLC's basic-program schools) and eight DA specialists for what was now the Directorate of Continuing Education (CE), leading to a revival of DA. In June 2006, the eight DA specialists assigned to CE were combined into a Diagnostic Assessment Center (DAC). DAC was mandated to follow a new model of DA development and training, combining existing DA protocol with the earlier concept of formative assessment based on individual learner variables. The resulting enhanced DA protocol generated a *learner profile* based on multiple parameters of individual learner variation, together with a *linguistic profile* based on a three-skill interview, yielding an LP following the model developed in 1998 forward.

DA training also followed a new model, using the DAC as a force multiplier to spread DA skills throughout DLIFLC. Instead of focusing primarily on development and delivery of DA services to CE, the DAC would develop both DA protocol and non-language-specific models of DA training, devoting most of its energy to training and certifying instructors from all languages and all DLIFLC teaching schools as DA specialists. The goal was "to turn 8 into 800," freeing schools from dependence on small teams of DA specialists and ensuring that DA would be conducted by the same instructors who taught the students.

The Enhanced Diagnostic Assessment Protocol

DA elicits and interprets data on multiple aspects of a learner's individual characteristics, relevant biographical detail, and proficiencies. Products include a profile of learner characteristics, profile of linguistic proficiencies and needs, and individualized LP. Together these provide an informed assessment of learners' current needs, to be updated as required.

DA is comprised of three stages: pre-interview data collection; three-skill interview; and post-interview follow-up, during which profiles are constructed and, based on them and in consultation with the learner, a tailored LP. At course completion, the learner becomes the author of the LP.

Pre-Interview Data Collection

Three forms of data are collected, bringing together social, psychological, and linguistic information. This portion of DA need not be repeated in subsequent iterations. First, a biographical questionnaire elicits information on aspects of learners' current situations and life history found historically to affect learning outcomes (e.g., Ehrman, 1996b, 164-172). Second, information is compiled on parameters of individuality relevant to the effectiveness of particular manners or modes of learning.

Personality type, as it affects learning contexts, modes, and tasks in which a learner will flourish, is assessed based on Jungian models (perhaps the best known of which are the Myers Briggs Type Indicator and Keirsey Temperament Sorter). DA training in this area is based on Leaver et al. (2005, Ch. 4, especially pp. 113ff.) and Ehrman (1996a).

Cognitive styles are assessed using the Ehrman and Leaver Learning Style Questionnaire Version 2.0 (E&L; cf. Ehrman, 1996b; Ehrman & Leaver, 2002, Leaver et al., 2005). E&L defines a global dichotomy of cognitive styles: *synopsis* vs. *ectasis*. *Ectenics* are learners who strive for conscious control over perception, information processing, and learning (i.e., a deliberative approach to learning), while *synoptics* are comfortable relying on less conscious or less controlled processing, willing to "trust their gut" (osmotic approach to learning; Ehrmann & Leaver, 2003, p. 395). The synopsis vs. ectasis dichotomy is articulated into 10 subordinate categories (cf. Table 1).

Synoptic Learning	Definition	Ectenic Learning	Definition
field independent	selects from context	field dependent	relies on context
field sensitive	learns by osmosis	field insensitive	learns by discrete item analysis
random	follows an internally developed order of processing	sequential	looks for an externally provided order of processing
global	focuses on the big picture	particular	focuses on the details
inductive	goes from examples to rule	deductive	goes from rule to examples

synthetic	prefers to assemble information into new wholes	analytic	disassembles wholes into constituent parts
analogue	metaphoric thinking	digital	linear thinking
concrete	interacts with the world directly and learns through application	abstract	interacts with the world through cognitive constructs and learns from formal rendition of knowledge
leveling	looks for similarities	sharpening	looks for disparities
impulsive	responds first	reflective	thinks first

Table 1. E&L Learning Styles Sub-Categories. Cited from Corin & Leaver (forthcoming).

Tolerance of ambiguity (in the sense described by Ehrman, 1999) is another parameter with profound implications for the forms of course organization in which learners may flourish or, conversely, fail regardless of capability and effort. This is discussed during DA training, but to date no feasible manner has been devised to encompass it systematically in DA protocol. Instead, tolerance for ambiguity is deduced or predicted from cognitive styles, relying on the untested assumption that they are correlated, or is elucidated through consultation with the student.

Sensory preferences. As generally acknowledged, learners differ in the ease or comfort with which they utilize various sensory channels (visual, auditory, tactile, kinesthetic) for processing information. A learner with strong visual preference and low auditory preference, for example, may be more comfortable learning from written (i.e., visualized) texts than from auditory (heard) texts, etc. Learners' sensory preferences are assessed using the Barsch Learning Style Inventory (Leaver & Oxford, 2001-2005, p. 87). An overview of this topic as it relates to second language acquisition, albeit focused on the VARK questionnaire, is Fleming and Mills (1992), which is used in DA specialist training.

Motivations. Alongside anecdotal information obtained through the biographical questionnaire, these are assessed using the Motivated Strategies for Learning Questionnaire (cf. Pintrich et al., 1991; Stoffa et al., 2011 on interpreting the MSLQ; Dörnyei & Csizér, 1998 has been used in DA training).

The results of this data collection are compiled in chart form, providing an easily interpretable approximate learner profile, which requires confirmation and adjustment through observation and consultation with the learner.

The third component of pre-interview data is an L2 writing sample composed without the use of linguistic reference materials, typically on a topic related to the learner's life history or future plans. Elicitation varies depending on a preliminary estimate of the learner's GLP. In addition to linguistic data instantiating areas of strength and weakness, the sample may provide information on motivations or learner variables beyond those elicited through other instruments. The writing sample is not a ratable sample. Rather, it is used much like the warm-up segment of an OPI—to provide assessors with a sample exemplifying the learner's current proficiency level and some specific strengths and weaknesses. It suggests an appropriate opening level for the DA interview and some areas to be probed during elicitation.

The Three-Skill DA Interview

The DA interview, as currently structured, consists of three components: listening, reading, speaking. Its goal is two-fold. First, it attempts to identify the learner's current GLP on an incremental scale based on the ILR, identifying a "floor" level of sustained performance and "ceiling" level (floor + .5) at which performance cannot be fully sustained. Second, it identifies and explores areas of weakness to be articulated and addressed through subsequent intervention. It focuses on learners' proximal learning potential, identifying tasks they can carry out with modest facilitation, in distinction to those they can carry out without facilitation and those they cannot carry out without extensive support.

The speaking interview is modeled on the structure of the ILR OPI but follows a distinct protocol reflecting the DA's formative (sympathetic) goal in contrast to the OPI's neutral summative assessment. It is comprised of the same inventory of tasks utilized in the OPI, ranging from *short questions* and *simple short conversation* to Level-4 tasks requiring intricate preludes: *abstract topic*, *support opinion* and *hypothesize*. However, where the OPI requires a strict protocol of alternating *level checks* (to establish/confirm the *floor*) and *probes* (to establish the *ceiling*), the formative purpose of the DA interview requires a greater emphasis on probes. In later portions of the interview probes may follow one another in succession, in order to explore as many areas of weakness as is feasible. Tasks assess learners' proficiency in terms of the same ILR performance domains as the OPI: global tasks and functions, text types produced, lexical control, structural control, delivery, sociolinguistic competence. Although the interview is not intended primarily to establish a reliable ILR level, the sample is rated, and experience with near-end-of-course DAs demonstrates that well-normed DA specialists typically assign ratings in close accord with OPI ratings assigned soon afterward.

For the reading interview, as indicated above, the DA specialist uses a packet of texts encompassing the full range of ILR levels, each text at a defined level verified by TT. The texts span a variety of topical domains, which may allow the specialist to identify areas of domain fossilization (in the sense of Ehrman, 2002 and CDLC, 2008, pp. 41-44) inhibiting achievement of upper ranges of proficiency. The comprehension questions associated with each text should be understood more broadly than the usual classroom sense; at higher levels they may probe comprehension of such attributes as non-explicit expression of authorial intent and authorial "voice."

The interview itself typically includes three or four texts, depending upon the course of the interview and the learner's fatigue level. It is adaptive, the level being adjusted up or down as required. So as to focus the assessment on reading (rather than oral) proficiency, the interview is conducted in English.

The listening interview follows the same pattern as the reading interview, based on a packet of TT-rated listening passages, each with its set of comprehension questions. Each text is played twice, and the learner may take notes.

Post-Interview Follow-Up

Post-interview feedback is based on two primary elements:

- *Learner profile*: pre-interview questionnaire results collated in chart form. This is accompanied by an overview based on quantitative and qualitative data.
- A *linguistic profile* of the learner's current proficiencies, indicating GLP but focusing on specific areas of weakness within the learner's ZPD. The GLP rating is one aspect of learners' proximal learning potential, and it is also a useful indicator of recent learning when DA is applied on successive occasions.

Based on the profiles, a tailored LP is compiled, then shared and explored with the learner during a post-interview consultation before finalization. A primary goal of the consultation is thus to fine-tune the LP, to help learners focus efforts to achieve their proximal learning potential. LPs should not be extensive but must go beyond broad generalizations to include actionable recommendations and may include benchmarks toward success and possibly a timeline. They may contain recommendations on two tracks—accommodation and confrontation, assisting learners to capitalize on their favored strategies, sensory channels, etc., while making them aware of alternatives and helping them to expand their repertoire of learning strategies. LPs may initially be composed by the DA specialist in collaboration with the learner, but by course conclusion they should be composed in L2 by the learner.

Beyond assisting learners to understand their proximal learning needs (i.e., for the immediate upcoming period), a second goal of the post-interview consultation is to discuss the learner profile (cognitive styles, sensory preferences, etc.) based on the evidence of both the questionnaires and three-skill interview. Questionnaires utilized in pre-interview data collection are far from infallible, so it is important to identify areas in which results are not in accord with observation or learners' beliefs.

All results are shared fully with all members of the instructional team and become the cornerstone on which tailoring of instruction will be based.

Finally, a class profile should be composed, revealing the predominant characteristics of the learner cohort and allowing instructors to tailor instruction based on predominant types with individualization to meet the needs of all. For example, a class with a high proportion of introvert ectenic learners may require more gradual work-up to stimulate performance in scenario-based activities. A class in which extrovert kinesthetic learners predominate may require adaptation of a program designed originally around content-based area studies emphasizing lengthy readings, individual analysis, and production in formalized genres such as diplomatic "requests for information."

Utilization of Diagnostic Assessment

Within DLIFLC's eight resident basic-program schools a variety of practices prevailed during the period through 2015, with a gradual trend away from individual as-needed application of DA toward systematic application. Within CE's School of Resident Education (RE),[21] DA was most thoroughly integrated into the learning process during the period 2006-2015, with systematic delivery of multiple iterations of DA in all courses. Remarks in this section focus on the RE's intermediate/advanced programs, with offerings in 8 languages as of 2015.

RE courses did not utilize textbooks. Curriculum was laid out in program/course descriptions and implemented primarily through content-based and scenario-based instruction using authentic materials (materials produced by, and for use by, native L2 speakers). Int/Adv courses ranged in length from 4-12 months,[22] with relatively few traditional quizzes and tests. DA thus bore much of the burden for in-course formative assessment. Except in the shortest (12-16 week) courses, students would have three DA iterations: at course outset, mid-point, and one month from completion.

Initial DA was particularly important in post-basic instruction. Students' linguistic profiles had diverged already during initial acquisition; subsequently they went on to a variety of other activities prior to their enrollment in CE courses, leading to further divergence of both the range and level of their proficiencies, resulting in a wide variety of class profiles.

Mid-point DA assessed progress toward learning objectives, set new baselines for GLP, specific knowledge, and proficiencies; identified major learning difficulties for intervention; and assisted in program correction.

Near-completion DA flagged any glaring lacunae requiring last-minute intervention, and students, in consultation with instructors, prepared their individualized LP for post-course learning. Since RE courses were conducted in L2 immersion mode throughout, the LP was composed in L2, reinforcing learners' confidence that they could utilize L2 to meet real-world needs. An LP compiled by the learner was also considered more likely to be implemented. Near-completion DA ratings that diverged significantly from out-going DLPT and OPI results were analyzed to determine what interventions or remedial actions might be required.

In addition to the three required iterations, all students (as indeed all DLIFLC students) who participate in overseas immersion programs underwent DA immediately before and after immersion. This assists in evaluation of an immersion's immediate benefit (bearing in mind that far from all learning benefits are measurable immediately upon return) and sets new baselines for learning following the "boost" the immersion hopefully provided. This is particularly important because Int/Adv immersion programs were content-based, conducted in a university (not a language-school) setting, and designed to simulate the

---

21. Since this article was drafted, the resident intermediate-advanced-course component of CE has been transferred to UGE.

22. Shorter courses (12-16 weeks) introduced in 2014 limited DA delivery to two instances per course.

experience of native-speaker university students studying the same topics. Such 2-4 week immersion programs commonly propelled well-prepared students over a GLP cusp with gains of .5 level for listening, reading, and speaking in as little as two weeks.

RE Instructors incorporated DA results into instruction in multiple ways. First, the breadth of learner characteristics and linguistic profiles was reflected in lesson planning through adaptation toward the cohort while ensuring individualization, breadth of activity types, variation of pace, etc., to meet all learners' needs. Second, DA results were a component of the detailed records that tracked each student's and class's progress. They were discussed at team meetings, used to plan intervention, were a crucial component of every course outcome analysis, and informed monthly individual student counseling. Finally, DA was a keystone of diagnosis and treatment of learning difficulties—the first item reviewed when CE academic specialists were called upon to assist in cases of particularly intractable difficulties.

Diagnostic Assessment Training

DA training has three primary goals. First, it creates and maintains a corps of DA specialists proficient in applying DA protocol. The second, broader, and arguably more important in the long run, is to enable DA trainees, in their day-to-day role as instructors, to better understand their students and more effectively facilitate their learning—developing their realization that classes are composed of learners with vastly differing profiles and needs and sensitizing them to strategies to more effectively address individual need. The third is to promote DA's purpose of helping instructors reduce attrition and profound learning frustration through a partnership of learners and learning facilitators (instructors and other support personnel).

DA trainees must master a range of conceptual components, including:

- dimensions of learner variation, how they interact to produce infinite composite profiles, and implications for the process and outcome of learning,
- the concept of proximal learning potential,
- the differential relevance of DA for initial acquisition and upper-range learning, and
- varieties of fossilization inhibiting achievement of near-native proficiency.

The last two areas reflect recent developments in training not yet fully implemented as of 2015. Training goes on to include skill sets beyond assessment of learner variables, including TT and elicitation, both of which require norming. DA practitioners must also understand intervention through both accommodation and confrontation, including composition of tailored LPs. Based on experience at both DLIFLC and the Foreign Service Institute (Betty Lou Leaver, personal communication), it has been estimated that about one year of practice is required for instructors to develop proficiency in the recognition and assessment of learner variables, elicitation, rating, and intervention necessary for effective formative assessment.

This breadth of topics and depth of training and norming has made it difficult to meet training objectives. This includes training enough DA specialists, training them to the point of proficiency, and keeping them sufficiently normed to provide reliable ratings, assessments of learner variables, diagnoses, and interventions. As a result, it has proven challenging to integrate DA as an integral component of all DLIFLC courses (especially in the much larger basic programs), much less to approach the goal of universal DA training for all instructors.

To address these challenges, the DAC experimented with various training models, initially 2-4 week intensive certification workshops, later blended media models combining asynchronous technology-mediated training with two three-day face-to-face norming workshops. Annual language-specific refresher and norming workshops for previously trained specialists were provided. The DAC simultaneously approached the broader goal of a DA-informed instructor corps through DA familiarization training for a larger number of instructors, initially through one-week workshops, later adding an online course.

Ultimately, the DAC adopted and began to implement a train-the-trainer (TtT) approach, distinguishing four levels of training. At the highest level, DAC staff required about a year of on-the-job performance to develop proficiency in training trainers. The second level was that provided by the DAC staff to prepare school-based DA trainers who would deliver DA specialist training (third level) to instructors in their respective schools. A fourth level—DA familiarization—was offered online by the DAC.

The DAC ultimately provided DA certification training to 509 instructors in 22 languages, certified 215 DA specialists (19 languages), and provided familiarization training to another 184 instructors (14 languages). Though a significant success, out of a faculty of almost 1,500 it was far from adequate when one considers faculty attrition, movement, and the ever-present requirement of refresher training. TtT should, in principle, allow a significant increase in this number, but the reality is more limited. On the one hand, TtT brings the danger of watering down training. On the other, aside from the issue of training resources there is also that of instructor resources. In the intense DLIFLC teaching environment, hours when instructors are not available for teaching or course/class preparation are difficult to budget, and DA training must compete for this time with yet other responsibilities, including numerous annual training requirements.

The overarching conclusion concerning DLIFLC's experience with DA through 2015 is that the process is highly effective when carried out systematically in all of its aspects. While its effects cannot be isolated from other factors, it is clearly one of several measures that resulted in a more than 50% increase in the percentage of Int/Adv students achieving proficiency requirements in all skills over the period 2006-2013. Despite these gains, the goal to universal application of DA and its benefits remains elusive.

Addressing the Effectiveness vs. Efficiency Dilemma

As articulated above, DA places heavy resource demands on all involved parties. Where insufficient training or short-cutting due to time pressure leads to inaccurate or generalized results or a failure to follow up on DA, the absence of positive results undermines confidence in DA on the part of students, instructors, and administrators alike. This creates a vicious circle, with schools or instructors reluctant to devote resources to DA and DA training. Insufficient awareness can also lead some instructors and managers to perceive DA as a last-gasp intervention technique to save students at risk, rather than a holistic approach to facilitating learning from day 1.

There are at least two related underlying tensions that contribute to this conundrum undermining DA's potential—one related to the instrument itself and the other to faculty training. First, the original DA design utilized "off-the-shelf" components that had been designed for testing purposes—OPI for speaking proficiency, and TT associated with level-rated content questions for reading and listening. This created a dichotomy between learning and formative assessment processes, through the use of instruments and procedures beyond those employed in the learning process *per se*. This tension can be addressed in part through redesign of DA protocol, which will be discussed below.

The second underlying tension derives from the first. Because DA involves instruments and procedures outside the learning process *per se*, additional training is required beyond that required for instructors to become proficient in facilitating learning (i.e., teaching). This additional training encompasses numerous concepts and techniques of practical application, more than can be covered comfortably in a limited workshop. It is more like a university program squeezed into a single workshop. Developing proficiency in DA implementation also requires extensive time-on-task.

The ultimate roots of these tensions are thus clear. On the one hand, DA training, involving as it does both formative assessment *per se* and exploitation/intervention based upon this assessment, should arguably be a central component of any L2 instructor training program. Viewed in this light, the fact that DA development and training as of 2015 were separate from the Instructor Certification Course taken by all new DLIFLC instructors would be one of the greatest impediments to the effective and efficient implementation of DA at DLIFLC. On the other hand, the fact that DA, though intended to inform the learning process, is carried out external to that process based in part on components designed for testing purposes, creates an inherent inefficiency in the use of DA. An effective strategy for resolving both of these tensions would thus involve redesigning DA to fully integrate protocol-based formative assessment (PBFA) as a component of the learning process *per se*, so that time devoted to PBFA is simultaneously time devoted to learning rather than subtracted from it. Only in this way can training for PBFA be integrated with IBFA into a holistic approach to instructor training uniting three essential components: 1) understanding the linguistic and extra-linguistic realities to be mastered, 2) understanding each student's individuality and the dynamics of learning cohorts, and 3) mastery of strategies and techniques to optimally facilitate learning by individual learners within their cohort.

Ideally, instructors should be able to evaluate each learner's unique learner and linguistic profile and respond to individual and cohort needs based on observation alone, without the need for PBFA. This level of proficiency is unlikely to be achieved by most instructors, so PBFA will continue to provide invaluable scaffolding, allowing instructors to gain a sufficient appreciation of their learners' needs and structure effective responses to those needs. DLIFLC therefore, as of 2015, followed a dual track approach to PBFA. The first was by a TtT approach to allow maximal access to existing DA. The second was a simultaneous effort to redesign DA itself with the goal of re-integrating DA into the learning process.

Redesigning Diagnostic Assessment

The goal of redesign was to move DA away from components rooted in testing modalities toward a structure designed for formative assessment as a component of the diagnostic instructional process. Instructors regularly practice *ad hoc* IBFA through every-day observations, optimizing support for learners through individualization while adapting group activities based on the profile and dynamic of the cohort. To maximize its effectiveness as well as its efficiency, DA must be maximally integrated with these day-to-day classroom IBFA processes.

The focus of the redesign was thus on the three-skill interview, the core of the linguistic assessment. The pre-interview data collection, in contrast, does not require class time; questionnaire results are easily quantifiable in chart form; and the writing sample is easily incorporated into the learning process. Post-interview processing is thus amenable to streamlining and, if DA can be carried out by any instructor, can be largely integrated into the instructional process.

As envisaged, re-design of the DA interview included four conceptual innovations:

1. expansion of text genres used in assessment,
2. utilization of multi-level texts,
3. RC and LC elicitation based on performance tasks rather than comprehension questions (based on the axiom that "a well-designed task cannot be completed without text comprehension;" "Thoughts for Thursday," 5 June 2014, DLIFLC Provost's Office), and
4. rating based on *proficiency cusp tables*, which require less training for effective use than ILR Level Descriptions.

Genre Expansion for Reading and Listening

As of 2015, internet news media were the main source of DA text selection, in part because DA was then limited to specific area-studies domains considered central for DLIFLC students, and relevant texts are readily available from these sources. Another reason is that one can readily find texts in these sources that are easily TT ratable (i.e., having a single unambiguous and consistent ILR level). In real life, however, texts typically do not fall neatly into discrete levels, and GLP in reading and listening requires the ability to process a broader range of genres and topics. Adherence to topical restrictions and TT guidelines provides a clear and transparent structure for DA but reduces the usefulness of materials for assessing GLP while increasing the difficulty of creating materials. The problem is thus that these selection criteria, useful in a testing environment, detract from the usefulness of DA for formative assessment.

Removing limitations on genres and topics:

- allows for assessment of a range of L/R proficiencies more truly representative of conditions encountered in real life (i.e., of true GLP),
- assists in the identification of domain fossilizations (in the sense of Ehrman, 2002; CDLC, 2008), and
- integrates DA with the learning process, since DA packets (texts and tasks) are selected using the same criteria as used in selecting authentic materials and tasks for classroom GLP development.

For assessment at higher levels, expansion of genres opens up an Eldorado of linguistic features available for analysis and interpretation, from simple grammatical structures to metaphor, nuance, hidden agendas, discourse virtuosity, diversity of voices and accents, etc. Expansion of genres also promotes thinking out of the box on the part of instructors/ DA specialists as opposed to following a script.

Genre expansion may encompass short stories, letters, diaries, social networks, poetic recitals, plays, excerpts from movies and talk shows, etc. To be sure, this broader range of text types requires more highly honed elicitation skills, but these are essentially the same skills as required for effective facilitation of classroom-based learning utilizing the same materials.

Multi-level passages vs multiple single-level passages

It has been observed over the course of many DA interviews that results can be skewed due to learner disorientation arising from discontinuity of content and assessment topics. This occurs when the assessor moves from one text to the next, with a different topic, level, and set of questions. This transition entails a discontinuity of cognitive processes, which can limit learners' performance and affect the assessor's interpretation of that performance. The skewed interpretation, in turn, can lead to the proposal of ineffective learning strategies.

Re-designed DA therefore used *multi-level texts* for assessing RC and LC, each united by a cohesive idea, but supporting tasks that require a variety of proficiency levels. The DA interview is adaptive and dynamic in nature, adjusting based on the flow of the interview. Elicitation based on multi-level texts allows assessors to adapt questions or tasks upward or downward without disorienting shifts in the learner's focus. This also allows for more natural deviations from the pre-set questions or tasks and should yield a more revealing interaction and accurate impressions. Multi-level texts are more representative of those typically encountered in real life, thus allowing for a more realistic assessment of GLP. Finally, use of multi-level texts makes it possible to decrease or eliminate TT training and periodic refresher norming.

Comprehension questions vs reading/listening performance tasks

The oral proficiency interview component of current DA is comprised of a regime of performance tasks, while the RC and LC interviews (like the DLPT) require learners to provide the most appropriate response to multiple-choice (MC) comprehension questions. Two tools with different potentials and limitations are thus applied to elicit samples from which the assessor will extract a unique interpretation. It is not known whether this disunity of method skews results, but at best it injects a further element of uncertainty into the assessment process.

MC questions, while arguably an effective tool for eliciting responses requiring particular levels of linguistic proficiency, are hardly analogous to typical real-life interactions with R/L texts and are therefore inappropriate for PBFA if it is to be maximally integrated with IBFA. Recent literature, for example Wiggleworth's (2008) survey, albeit focused more on summative assessment, lends general yet critical support to the claim that on the road to GLP, "reading tasks and assessments should mirror real-world uses of reading" (Davis, n.d.) and, of course, listening. Re-designed DA thus assessed R/L through performance tasks, with the caveat that in assessing GLP one cannot fully observe a distinction (noted by Wigglesworth, 2008) between focus on successful task performance vs. focus on the elicited linguistic sample. Task-based assessment is expected to provide a truer appreciation of learners' proficiencies, both in level and particulars, while overcoming any deleterious effects of the current methodological inconsistency. Tasks can include generating or answering questions; non-linguistic tasks; filling out charts, grids, or semantic maps; indicating structural aspects of the text; providing meta-cognitive judgments; and product-oriented tasks. In other words, they can span the range of tasks that an instructor might otherwise use for learning purposes. Mastery of required elicitation skills should therefore require only modest training beyond that required for effective task-based classroom instruction (e.g., in gradated facilitation to achieve the dynamic aspect of assessment), and largely bridge the gap between interview and the classroom.

A third advantage of the task-based approach is that, unlike comprehension questions, performance tasks allow for observation of the learner's cognitive styles, strategies, etc. in action. This supplements data elicited by questionnaire and consultation, thus assisting the assessor in providing a more useful individualized LP.

For rating purposes, one or more tasks will be provided at each ILR level supported by a given text. To maximize their effectiveness for rating purposes, they will be applied in an alternating pattern of level checks and probes, as in the OPI elicitation regime.

Streamlining DA Reference Materials

Within the pre-existing DA protocol, assessment of GLP level requires DA specialists to apply a set of reference charts entitled "Description of Performance by ILR Level" for the various skills, performance domains, and levels encompassed by the ILR. These are applied to the sample elicited during the DA interviews to compile some 12-14 pages of calibrated ratings and feedback. This requires detailed knowledge of the descriptions for various skills, performance domains and levels, as well as intensive norming and periodic refresher training both for elicitation skills and rating. When carried out comprehensively, the process can be sufficiently lengthy that results no longer seem fresh when shared with the student and teaching team; when this occurs, enthusiasm to apply the fruits of the effort may have dissipated.

Re-design of DA required an assessment reference tool that is cohesive and user-friendly, yet retains or increases depth of substance, reflecting multiple parameters of linguistic performance. It was decided that the most promising approach—simplest yet most comprehensive and nuanced—was through what have become known as *proficiency cusp tables.* These are created by translating the criteria from the various ILR performance domains (lexical, structural, socio-linguistic competence, etc.) into language-specific tables of "can do" statements for particular abilities at particular ILR levels. These in turn are based on an unpublished non-language-specific draft developed under the auspices of the National Foreign Language Center and entitled "Proficiency Cusp Tables or the Generic Learning Profiles (GLPs) for Reading and Listening" (Betty Lou Leaver, personal communication; see now Leaver, this volume). This instrument dissects linguistic performance into 10 multi-dimensional categories not limited strictly to ILR. Categories relevant to formative assessment of GLP beyond ILR include "Strategic and Emotional Competence" and "Attentional Focus." The cusp tables are associated with answers and keys for determining the profile of a learner in a granulated manner. Through their categories, they prompt DA specialists/instructors concerning perspectives from which enhancement of a learner's performance can be approached. This approach was in fact adopted by earlier DA developers, and cusp tables developed for several languages. However, the approach was dropped, presumably because resources were not available for development of cusp tables at all proficiency levels for all DLIFLC languages.

Cusp tables have deficiencies which must be addressed before they can be generally applied as the basis for assessing GLP. Several LC categories are incomplete, and there are at present no speaking and writing tables. Until the latter are developed, ILR level descriptions must remain in use. Cusp tables might first be applied for LC/RC, the difference in criteria corresponding to the dichotomy productive vs. receptive skills.

8.5. Assessing Components of Redesigned DA

The new approach to DA underwent its first trial applications for Arabic, Chinese, English, Korean, Russian, and Spanish, using post-basic students (ILR 2-3) as subjects. The trial assessments were carried out within the context of a DA Summit held in February 2015. The trial DAs employed multi-level texts, expanded genres, and task-based elicitation. Cusp tables were not employed, rating and analysis being based on ILR level descriptions. Overall, the three components that were tested were positively evaluated.

Use of multi-level texts was positively assessed by both learners and assessors, as this brought the assessment process closer to the classroom learning process, while allowing for the identification of learners' strengths and weaknesses. The assessors also appreciated the fact that multi-level texts eliminate the need for cumbersome TT. Nevertheless, use of multi-level texts for assessment raised one unanticipated challenge. Multi-level texts tended to be longer, which in turn increased the role of memory vis-à-vis proficiency as factors limiting performance, necessitating compensatory strategies in formulating tasks and questions (e.g., drawing attention to particular portions of a text). However, it was also noted that any increased "cognitive load" of multi-level texts also increases opportunities to observe cognitive styles, which is desirable for formative assessment.

Use of expanded genres was positively evaluated by learners, who perceived the experience as a refreshing expansion of their learning into new areas.

Task-based elicitation was assessed as being useful for identifying specific strengths and weaknesses. Learners' cognitive styles and strategies, moreover, were observable during the task-based assessment process, as was anticipated, so that the interviews complemented learner-profile data elicited by questionnaire. A further advantage that had not been anticipated was that weaknesses in socio-cultural proficiency emerged far more clearly in some instances than would have been the case using comprehension questions.

Task-based assessment of GLP level proved a greater challenge. It was felt that in future trials the levels of the tasks provided for each text should be made more transparent. The use of cusp tables is also expected to mitigate this difficulty, as they provide exemplification of performance characteristic at particular proficiency levels. By the same token, cusp tables should also make it easier to design tasks.

Though use of English for elicitation was retained in the task-based R/L assessment—considered a necessary evil for rating purposes—interview teams believed that this artifact of the testing environment detracted from the goal of integrating PBFA into the learning process. This was especially true for the post-basic student subjects in the trial DAs. Accurate assessment of reading and listening proficiencies without use of English requires techniques to isolate learners' proficiencies in listening and reading from those in speaking, so that deficiencies in the latter do not mask proficiencies in the former.

In some trial interviews the dynamic aspect of assessment was achieved: it became clear whether the learner was "close to," or "far from," the ability to independently complete a task. To ensure that this occurs and provide a dynamic aspect of quantification or gradation to the rating process, a schedule of graded levels of scaffolding (support or hints) might be prepared for each task, roughly along lines suggested by Aljaafreh and Lantolf's (1994) "Regulatory Scale" of mediation.

The re-designed DA with task-based elicitation, multi-level texts, and expanded range of genres was positively evaluated by all student subjects, all of whom had previous experience with the pre-existing DA. They were animated by the process, in part because the tasks engaged higher-order learning skills, and in part because they were actually learning. Beyond the knowledge gained from manipulating textual content, they were becoming aware of specific limitations in their proficiency and overcoming some on the spot, so that they ended interviews with greater knowledge or proficiency than they possessed at the start. Interview teams for the various languages also agreed with this assessment.

It was agreed that future trials of re-designed DA should utilize cusp tables, at least for those languages and skills for which they are available, as it was anticipated that this would significantly facilitate analysis and GLP rating.

In conclusion, the three "cornerstones" of re-designed DA that were tested—genre expansion, multi-level texts, and task-based elicitation—received a generally favorable evaluation, with suggestions for improvement. The greatest remaining challenge was in the measurement of performance, the answer to which lies in the fourth cornerstone—language-specific proficiency cusp tables as reference tools.

Conclusions

DA is a highly effective PBFA tool for enhancing learning outcomes when fully and proficiently applied. However, as the scale of its employment increases, DA's usefulness tends to decrease due to issues of efficiency. These derive from two primary sources. The first is the existing instrument, which is time-consuming and laborious to apply, and is conducted outside the learning process. The second is the scope of the training and training maintenance required for effective application. Both difficulties derive in part from the roots of DA's linguistic assessment components in the field of testing.

In order to achieve DLIFLC's vision of providing all students with multiple iterations of PBFA, fully integrated within the learning process with IBFA, re-design of DA is required. The goal would be a continuous dynamically oriented assessment of each learner, establishing a baseline learner profile and linguistic profile, then tracking these through observation, "re-setting" the LP periodically based on subsequent DA iterations.

A more distant goal is the full integration of formative assessment into the learning process through IBFA alone, by instructors who possess the skills to apply DA's components spontaneously and intuitively in day-to-day instructional activities. In the real world, that goal is difficult to attain. In college/university contexts, L2 instructors often have backgrounds and ongoing activities in other fields. In the DLIFLC context as well, alongside instructors with degrees preparing them specifically for L2 instruction, many others bring valuable experiences in other fields to their positions, receiving cross-training at DLIFLC to become effective language instructors. In such an environment and given DLIFLC's need to process thousands of learners simultaneously year-round with accountability for attainment of proficiency goals and requirements, it is unlikely that the "interventionist" PBFA approach can be entirely superseded. The practical goal must therefore be a maximally effective and efficient combination of PBFA and IBFA through a streamlined DA.

References

Aljaafreh, A., and Lantolf, J.P. (1994). Negative feedback as regulation and second language learning in the zone of proximal development. *Modern Language Journal 78*, 465–483. https://doi.org/10.1111/j.1540-4781.1994.tb02064.x

Bernhardt, E.B., & James, C.J. (1987). The teaching and testing of comprehension in foreign language learning. In D.W. Birckbichler (Ed.), *Proficiency, policy and professionalism in foreign language education* (pp. 65–81). Lincolnwood: National Textbook Company.

Child, J.R. (1987). Language proficiency levels and the typology of texts. In H. Byrnes & M. Canale (Eds.), *Defining and developing proficiency: Guidelines, implementations, and concepts* (pp. 97–106). Lincolnwood: National Textbook Company.

Coalition of Distinguished Language Centers (CDLC). (2008). *What works: Helping students reach native-like second-language competence.* Hollister: MSI Press.

Corin, A.R. & Leaver, B.L. (forthcoming). *Fields of the Mind: History, Theory, & Application of Cognitive Field Concepts to Language Learning.* Hollister: MSI Press.

Davis, R.L. (n.d.). Reading performance tasks. (http://pages.uoregon.edu/rldavis/readingtasks/whyperformance.html).

Dörnyei, Z. (1994). Motivation and motivating in the foreign language classroom. *Modern Language Journal 78*(3), 273–284.

Dörnyei, Z., & Csizér, K. (1998). Ten commandments for motivating language learners: Results of an empirical study. *Language Teaching Research 2*(3), 203–229.

Ehrman, M. (1996a). Learners and teachers: The application of psychology to second language acquisition. *Russian Language Journal 55,* 33–71.

Ehrman, M. (1996b). *Understanding second language learning difficulties.* Thousand Oaks: Sage.

Ehrman, M. (1999). Ego boundaries and tolerance of ambiguity in second language learning. In J. Arnold (Ed.), *Affect in language learning* (pp. 68–86). Cambridge: Cambridge University Press.

Ehrman, M. (2002). The learner at the superior-distinguished threshold. In B.L. Leaver & B. Shekhtman (Eds.), *Developing professional-level language proficiency* (pp. 245–259). Cambridge University Press.

Ehrman, M., & Leaver, B.L. (2002). *E&L learning style questionnaire v. 2.0.* (2002). http://www.cambridge.org/resources/0521837510/2127_Leaver%20learning%20styles%20test.DOC

Ehrman, M., & Leaver, B.L. (2003). Cognitive styles in the service of language learning. *System 31,* 393–415.

Fleming, N.D., & Mills, C. (1992). Not another inventory, rather a catalyst for reflection. *To Improve the Academy 11,* 137–149.

Lantolf, J.P., & Thorne, S.L. (2006). Sociocultural theory and second language acquisition. In B. VanPatten & J. Williams (Eds.), *Theories in second language acquisition* (pp. 201–224). Mahwah: Erlbaum.

Leaver, B.L. (1997). *Teaching the whole class.* Thousand Oaks: Corwin.

Leaver, B.L., Ehrman, M., & Lekic, M. (2004). Distinguished-level learning online: Support materials from LangNet and RusNet. *Foreign Language Annals 37*(4), 556–565.

Leaver, B.L., Ehrman, M., & Shekhtman, B. (2005). *Achieving success in second language acquisition.* Cambridge: Cambridge University Press.

Leaver, B.L., & Oxford, R. (2001-2005). Individual difference theory in faculty development: What faculty developers should know about style. *Russian Language Journal 55,* 73–127.

Pintrich, P.R., Smith, D.A.F, Garcia, T., & McKeachie, W.J. (1991). *A manual for the use of the Motivated Strategies for Learning Questionnaire (MSLQ).* National Center for Research to Improve Post-Secondary Teaching and Learning (U. of Michigan), http://files.eric.ed.gov/fulltext/ED338122.pdf

Poehner, M.E. (2008). *Dynamic assessment: A Vygotskian approach to understanding and promoting L2 Development.* Springer.

Stoffa, R., Kush, J.C., & Heo, M. (2011). Using the Motivated Strategies for Learning Questionnaire and the Strategy Inventory for Language Learning in assessing motivation and learning strategies of generation 1.5 Korean immigrant students. *Education Research International* 2011, 8 pages. Article ID 491276

Wigglesworth, G. (2008). Task and performance based assessment. In Elana Shohamy (Ed.), *Language Testing and Assessment* (2nd ed., pp. 111–122). Springer.

About the Authors

Andrew R. Corin is Professor Emeritus at the Defense Language Institute Foreign Language Center. He is former Dean of DLIFLC's School of Resident Post-Basic Education, also former Dean of Educational Support Services for Post-Basic Education. His primary languages of teaching are Serbian-Croatian and Russian.

Currently a military interpreter of Ukrainian, stationed abroad, Sergey Entis is Academic Specialist (retired) at the Defense Language Institute Foreign Language Center, where he made contributions for several years as the Diagnostic Assessment Center Director and as Senior Academic Advisor to the Provost. His primary languages of teaching are Russian and Ukrainian.

ABSTRACTS

Abstracts in Chinese

Translated by Dr. Yalun Zhou, Rensselaer Polytechnical Institute

超越语言: 辩论作为高强度文化参与和领导力的外语教学手段

Emilie Cleret (French War College)

本文讨论了巴黎法国战争学院的高级专业军事教育（PME）中使用辩论来帮助军官达到类似母语的英语语言能力。

在法国，高级专业军事教育由两所学校提供--法国战争学院（Ecole de Guerre）和高等军事研究中心（Centre des hautes études militaires）。本文探讨的案例是在法国战争学院为期一年的课程中，英语研究系利用辩论来帮助军官学员们达到类似于二级母语水平的语言能力。作为领导这个系的践行者，作者探讨了辩论课的课程设计及教师管理以达到预期目标。该系的所有成员都来自于英语国家。

关键词: 辩论、领导力、(法国)军事教育、文化、论证、公共演讲

帮助学习者达到优异级语言水平

James E. Bernhardt, Ph.D. (Foreign Service Institute, emeritus)

本文提出，所有已经达到优秀水平并希望达到优异水平的语言学习者都有一个共同的任务，那就是需要将他们的词汇量增加一倍。文章建议，优异级语言水平培训的教学设计应包括大量的输入：阅读、听和看。文章还提出了一些评估学习材料是否符合学习者水平的方法，这些方法都是以词汇为基础的，并主张学习材料要适合学习者的个人需求、目标和兴趣。

本文作者仔细研究了培养高水平语言学习者项目的目标，并指出并非所有努力达到优异级水平的学习者都有相同的最终目标。在这个层次上，他们的目标因学习者而异。该目标和资助他们学习的培训机构的需求也肯定不同于ACTFL标准和ILR技能水平描述中所描述的优异级水平的特征。及：口才好，是受过良好教育人群中的一员，并且能够以接近书面语的方式说话。

文章宣称，学生在学习中有一系列的权利，当他们行使这些权利时，甚至可以在中途改变每门课程的课程走向。不同于通用的布鲁姆分类法，本文作者研究了语言培训项目通往成功的途径，建议使用设计思维方式来创建一个语言教学项目，注重评估培训材料是否适当，特别关注单词、单词家族，以及注重了解学习者本人的词库大小和阅读速度。

当教师很了解他们的学习者时，他们可以与学习者和利益相关者合作，为每个学习者制定符合其确切需求的学习计划。

关键词：词汇、目标、权利、布鲁姆分类法、文本分析

通往口语优异水平的路线图

Jack Franke (Defense Language Institute Foreign Language Center)

尽管在美国留学被视为必要条件，但留学经历并不是达到优异级外语口语水平的万能药。 本研究试图揭示毅力、留学、动机和学习者的自主性是如何在获取优异级的口语能力方面发挥作用的。 利用复杂性理论和现象学设计的理论框架，本研究采访了美国西部一所大学的四位教育工作者。 通过访谈和文献研究，作者调查了成功的外语教育者为达到优异级的口语教学水平所使用的路线图。对参与者的访谈数据分析显示，优异级的口语能力是一种高度个人化的追求，其特点是基于不同的动机：有对外语的选择、对目标文化的参与、毅力和时间投入。 总的来说，参与者是高度自我有效（self-efficacious）的学习者，许多人与说外语的配偶结婚，并在外国文化和社区中度过了很长时间。 这项研究为那些希望达到近母语外语口语水平的学生和教育工作者提供了可以借鉴的路线图。

关键词：优异级语言水平、毅力、出国留学、动机

语言水平升级：基于最接近发展区的形成性评估指南

Betty Lou Leaver, Ph.D. (MSI Press LLC)

各个外语水平的级别(ILR-1, -2, -3, -4/ACTFL 初级，中级，高级，优级)之间差距很大，而跨越不同语言等级之间的技能可能需要很多年的时间。对于某些四级语言使用者来说，这个时间段可能高达17年。在美国国家外语中心的支持下，本文作者参考借鉴了大量优秀级语言水平(Level-4)使用者的意见， 开发了语言水平临界点升级(Cusp Grids)指南。该指南根据个体学习者的最接近发展区 (ZPD)，并结合形成性评估来确定个体学习者从一个外语水平等级上升到另一个水平等级所需要熟练掌握的关键语言技能以及达到下一个更高语言水平应该采取的最佳学习步骤。目前为英、法、俄、西班牙语设计的突破临界点表格式指南可用于指导其他语种类似指南的开发。

关键词：语言水平临界点；临界点水平升级指南，最接近发展区，形成性评估，语言熟练水平

基于协议的形成性评估：国防语言学院的发展和变革

Andrew R. Corin, Ph. D. (Defense Language Institute Foreign Language Center, emeritus) & Sergey Entis (Defense Language Institute Foreign Language Center, retired)

基于协议的形成性评估（PBFA）可以成为一个加强学习和诊断学习困难的强有力的工具。然而，在实施PBFA的过程中，效力和效率之间存在着固有的矛盾。这可以通过多种策略来解决。比如说将PBFA "定量配给 "有学习困难的个别学生或者在少数情况下，将PBFA应用于所有的学生；或者在协议中设计更高的效率。无论采用哪种策略，人们都认为基于协议的形成性评估(PBFA)应该最大限度地与基于教学的形成性评价（IBFA）相结合，

作为日常课堂教学的一个组成部分。本文阐述了1989年至2015年期间国防语言学院外语中心（DLIFLC）所面临的困境，以及通过重新设计PBFA来克服这一困境的历程。

关键词： 诊断评估；形成性评估；动态评估；最接近发展区；学习者变量；学习风格；文本类型学；语言能力；世界语言教育；外语学习；国防语言学院外语中心

Abstracts in English

Beyond the Language: Debating as High-Intensity Cultural Engagement & Leadership

Emilie Cleret (French War College, Paris)

This article discusses the use of debating in senior professional military education (PME) at the French War College in Paris to help officers reach native-like English language competence.

In France, senior Professional Military Education (PME) is delivered by two schools – Ecole de Guerre (French War College) and Centre des hautes études militaires, (Centre for Higher Military Studies). This article explores the use of debating by the English Studies Department to support the officers' effort to achieve a native-like level of L2 competence during their one-year course in the French War College. The author's perspective is that of a practitioner who heads this department, designs the courses, and manages the faculty that delivers them. All the members of the faculty are from English-speaking countries.

Keywords: Debating, Leadership, (French) Military Education, Culture, Argumentation, Public Speaking

Helping Learners Achieve the Distinguished Level of Proficiency

James E. Bernhardt, Ph.D. (Foreign Service Institute, emeritus)

This article proposes that a task all learners who have attained superior levels of proficiency and who wish to achieve the distinguished level have in common is the need to double the size of their vocabulary. The article suggests that instructional designs for distinguished level training should include massive amounts of input: reading, listening, and watching. It also proposes a number of ways, all vocabulary based, to evaluate whether materials are at-level for learners and advocates for materials that are appropriate to the individual learners' needs, objectives and interests.

The article takes a close look at the goals of higher-level programs and notes that not all learners working towards distinguished levels of proficiency have the same end goals in mind. Their objectives, at this level, differ from learner to learner. Their objectives and the needs of the organizations that fund their training also surely differ from the characteristics of distinguished level proficiency implied by the ACTFL standards and the ILR skill level descriptions: eloquence, membership in the cloistered elect of the well-educated, and the ability to speak in ways that approximate written texts.

The article asserts that students have a set of rights, which, when exercised, may change the trajectory of each course even midstream. It examines paths towards success, rejecting the use of Bloom's taxonomy and suggesting the use of design thinking approaches to creating an instructional program. Attention is paid to techniques for evaluating the appropriateness of materials for training, with a special focus on words, word families, and the importance of knowing the size of a learner's word bank and speed at which the student reads.

When instructors know their learners well, they can, working with the learners and stakeholders, create a learning plan for each learner which meets their precise needs.

Key words: vocabulary, objectives, rights, Bloom's taxonomy, text profiling

Roadmaps to Distinguished Speaking Proficiency

Jack Franke (Defense Language Institute Foreign Language Center)

Although study abroad is viewed in the United States as *sine qua non*, the study abroad experience is not a panacea to achieve distinguished foreign language speaking proficiency. This study attempts to uncover how persistence, study abroad, motivation, and learner autonomy play into the pursuit of distinguished speaking proficiency. Using the theoretical framework of complexity theory and phenomenological design, the study utilizes interviews of four educators at an institute in the Western United States as the primary instrument of data collection. This study investigates the roadmaps which successful foreign language educators have utilized to achieve distinguished speaking proficiency through interviews and documentary research. Data analysis of interviews with the participants reveals distinguished speaking proficiency was a highly personal pursuit characterized by different motivations based on the choice of a foreign language, engagement in the target culture, grit, and time. Overall, the participants were highly self-efficacious learners, many married to foreign-speaking spouses, who spent extended periods in the foreign culture and community. The study provided possible roadmaps for students and educators who wish to achieve near-native speaking proficiency in a foreign language.

Keywords: persistence, study abroad, motivation, learner autonomy, distinguished speaking proficiency, motivation

On the Cusp: Tables to Guide Formative Assessment Incorporating Zone of Proximal Development Consideration

Betty Lou Leaver, Ph.D. (MSI Press LLC)

The chasm between the various proficiency levels (ILR -1, -2, -3, 4/ACTFL Novice, Intermediate, Advanced, Distinguished) is large. Traversing the space between the levels can take many years—up to 17 years for some Level-4 language users. The Cusp Grids, developed under the guise of the National Foreign Language Center with input from large numbers of Level-4 language users, focus on the proficiency elements critical from passing from one level to another and how to use this knowledge along with formative assessment to determine best next steps for individual learners, based on their zones of proximal development (Vygotsky). The grids provided for English, French, Russian, and Spanish can be used to guide the development of similar grids for other languages.

Keywords: proficiency cusps, cusp grids, zone of proximal development, formative assessment, proficiency levels

Protocol-Based Formative Assessment: Evolution and Revolution at the Defense Language Institute

Andrew R. Corin, Ph. D. (Defense Language Institute Foreign Language Center, emeritus) & Sergey Entis (Defense Language Institute Foreign Language Center, retired)

Protocol-based formative assessment (PBFA) can be a powerful tool for enhancing learning and diagnosing learning challenges. Yet there is an inherent tension between effectiveness and efficiency in the delivery of PBFA. This can be addressed through a variety of strategies: "rationing" PBFA to instances of individual learning difficulties, applying PBFA to all students but in fewer instances, or by engineering greater efficiency into the protocol. Regardless of the strategy adopted, it is taken for granted that PBFA should be maximally integrated with instruction-based formative assessment (IBFA) as an integral component of day-to-day classroom instruction. This article articulates the dilemma as it developed at the Defense Language Institute Foreign Language Center (DLIFLC) between 1989 and 2015 and the path pursued to overcome it through re-design of PBFA.

Keywords: diagnostic assessment; formative assessment; dynamic assessment; zone of proximal development; learner variables; learning styles; text typology; language proficiency; world language education; foreign language learning; Defense Language Institute Foreign Language Center

Abstracts in French

Jérôme Collin

Au-delà du langage : Le *debating* au service d'un engagement culturel de haute intensité et du leadership

Emilie Cleret (Ecole de guerre, Paris)

Cet article traite de l'utilisation du *debating* dans le cadre de l'Enseignement militaire supérieure (EMS) à l'Ecole de guerre de Paris pour aider les officiers à atteindre une compétence linguistique en anglais semblable à celle d'un locuteur natif.

En France, l'Enseignement militaire supérieure (EMS) est dispensée par deux écoles – l'Ecole de Guerre et le Centre des hautes études militaires. Le cas étudié par cet article concerne l'utilisation du *debating* par le Département langue anglaise pour soutenir les efforts des officiers afin qu'ils puissent atteindre pendant leur formation d'un an à l'Ecole de guerre un niveau de compétence en L2 semblable à celui d'un natif. La perspective de l'auteur est celle d'un praticien qui dirige ce département, conçoit les cours et gère le corps enseignant qui les dispense. Tous les membres du corps professoral sont originaires de pays anglophones.

Mots-clés: *Debating*, leadership, éducation militaire (française), culture, argumentation, prise de parole.

Aider les apprenants à atteindre un très haut niveau de compétence

James E. Bernhardt, Ph.D. (*Foreign Service Institute*, émérite)

Le présent article propose que tous les apprenants qui ont atteint niveau avancé de compétence et qui souhaitent atteindre un très haut niveau ont en commun la nécessité de doubler la taille de leur vocabulaire. L'article suggère que les modèles pédagogiques pour la formation au très haut niveau devraient inclure une quantité massive d'éléments lexicaux pour améliorer les compétences réceptives (textes, audio et vidéo). Il propose également un certain nombre de méthodes, toutes basées sur le vocabulaire, pour évaluer si les supports sont au niveau des apprenants, et préconise des supports adaptés aux besoins, aux objectifs et aux intérêts de chaque apprenant.

L'article examine de près les objectifs des programmes de haut niveau et note que tous les apprenants qui travaillent à l'obtention de très hauts niveaux de compétence n'ont pas les mêmes objectifs finaux en tête. Leurs objectifs, à ce niveau, diffèrent d'un apprenant à l'autre. Leurs objectifs ainsi que les besoins des organisations qui financent leur formation diffèrent aussi nettement des caractéristiques de la compétence de très haut niveau décrites par les normes de l'ACTFL et par les descripteurs des niveaux de compétence de l'ILR : éloquence, appartenance au cercle restreint des élites et capacité à parler d'une manière qui se rapproche du style écrit.

L'article affirme que les étudiants ont un ensemble de droits qui, lorsqu'ils sont exercés, peuvent changer la trajectoire de chaque cours, à tout moment de la formation. Il examine les voies de la réussite, en rejetant l'utilisation de la taxinomie de Bloom et en suggérant l'utilisation de modélisations pour créer un programme d'enseignement. Une attention particulière est accordée aux techniques d'évaluation de la pertinence du matériel de formation, avec un accent particulier mis sur le lexique, les familles lexicale et l'importance de connaître la quantité d'éléments lexicaux que possède l'apprenant, ainsi que sa vitesse de lecture.

Lorsque les formateurs connaissent bien leurs apprenants, ils peuvent, en collaboration avec ces derniers et les intervenants, créer un plan d'apprentissage qui réponde aux besoins précis de chaque apprenant.

Mots clés: vocabulaire, objectifs, droits, taxinomie de Bloom, profilage de textes

Feuilles de route pour l'acquisition d'une expression orale de très haut niveau.

Jack Franke (Defense Language Institute Foreign Language Center)

Bien que les études en immersion soient considérées aux États-Unis comme une condition *sine qua non* à l'apprentissage d'une langue étrangère, les études à l'étranger ne constituent pas pour autant la panacée pour atteindre un très haut niveau en compétence orale. Cette étude cherche à découvrir comment la persévérance, les études en immersion, la motivation et l'autonomie de l'apprenant jouent un rôle dans la quête d'une compétence orale de très haut niveau. Dans le cadre de la théorie de la complexité et du modèle phénoménologique, l'étude a utilisé, comme principal instrument de collecte de données, des entretiens avec quatre éducateurs dans un institut de l'Ouest des États-Unis. Cette étude a examiné, à l'aide d'entretiens et de recherches documentaires, les feuilles de route qu'ont utilisées des enseignants de langues étrangères ayant réussi à atteindre une compétence d'expression orale de très haut niveau. L'analyse des données issues des entretiens avec les participants a révélé que la maîtrise de l'expression orale était une quête très personnelle, caractérisée par différentes motivations reposant sur le choix d'une langue étrangère, l'engagement dans la culture cible, la détermination et le temps. Dans l'ensemble, les participants étaient des apprenants autonomes et efficaces; beaucoup étaient mariés à des conjoints parlant une langue étrangère et passaient de ce fait de longues périodes dans la culture et la communauté correspondantes. L'étude a fourni des feuilles de route pouvant inspirer les étudiants et les éducateurs qui souhaitent atteindre une compétence linguistique proche de celle des locuteurs natifs.

Mots clés: ténacité, immersion, motivation, autonomie de l'apprenant, compétence linguistique de haut très niveau

Sur la corde raide : Grilles pour guider l'évaluation formative en tenant compte de la zone de développement proximal

Betty Lou Leaver, Ph.D. (MSI Press LLC)

L'abîme entre les différents niveaux de compétence (ILR 1, 2, 3, 4/ACTFL Débutant, Intermédiaire, Avancé, Très haut niveau) est grand ; Passer d'un niveau à un autre peut prendre de nombreuses années – jusqu'à 17 ans pour certains locuteurs de langue de niveau 4. Les grilles « Cusp », développées sous l'égide du *National Foreign Language Center*, avec la contribution d'un grand nombre de locuteurs de langues de niveau 4, se concentrent sur les éléments de compétence essentiels pour passer d'un niveau à l'autre et sur la manière d'utiliser ces connaissances, ainsi que sur l'évaluation formative, afin de déterminer les étapes successives les mieux adaptées à chaque apprenant individuel, en fonction de ses zones de développement proximal. Les grilles fournies pour l'anglais, le français, le russe et l'espagnol peuvent être utilisées pour guider le développement de grilles similaires pour d'autres langues.

Mots clés: grilles « Cusp » de compétence, grilles « Cusp », zone de développement proximal, évaluation formative, niveaux de compétence.

Évaluation Formative sur Protocole : Évolution et révolution au Defense Language Institute

Andrew R. Corin, Ph. D. (*Defense Language Institute Foreign Language Center*, émérite) & Sergey Entis (*Defense Language Institute Foreign Language Center*, retraité)

L'Évaluation Formative sur Protocole peut être un outil puissant pour améliorer l'apprentissage et en diagnostiquer les difficultés. Cependant, il existe une tension inhérente entre l'efficacité et l'efficience dans la mise en œuvre de l'Évaluation Formative sur Protocole. Cette tension peut être abordée par le biais d'une grande variété de stratégies : «rationner « l'Évaluation Formative sur Protocole en fonction des difficultés d'apprentissage individuelles ; appliquer l'Évaluation Formative sur Protocole à tous les élèves, mais dans un moins grand nombre de cas ; ou élaborer un protocole d'une plus grande efficacité. Quelle que soit la stratégie adoptée, il va de soi que l'Évaluation Formative sur Protocole doit être intégrée au maximum à une évaluation formative basée sur l'enseignement en tant que partie intégrante de l'enseignement quotidien en classe. Cet article présente le dilemme tel qu'il s'est développé au *Defense Language Institute Foreign Language Center* (DLI-FLC) entre 1989 et 2015, ainsi que la voie suivie pour le surmonter par une nouvelle conception de l'Évaluation Formative sur Protocole.

Mots-clés: évaluation diagnostique; évaluation formative; évaluation dynamique; zone de développement proximal; variables de l'apprenant; styles d'apprentissage; typologie des textes; compétences linguistiques ; enseignement des langues du monde; apprentissage des langues étrangères; Defense Language Institute Foreign Language Center.

Abstracts in German

Gerd Brendel

Mehr als Sprache: Debattieren als High Intensity Kulturabtausch und Leadership

Emilie Cleret (French War College)

Dieser Artikel beschreibt den Gebrauch des Debattierens als Teil der Fortgeschrittenen Militaerfortbildung (PME) an den zwei Militaerschulen, dem French War College und dem Center for Higher Military Studies. Die Fortbildung am War College in Paris unterstuetzt die Englisch Studien der Offiziere mit dem Ziel einer fast muttsprachlichen Sprachkompetenz im Englischen.

Dieser Artikel untersucht den Gebrauch des Debattierens im Englischunterricht zur Unterstuetzung des Ereichens einer fast muttersprachlichen Kompetenz waehrend des ein-jaehrigen Studiums am War College. Die Perspekive der Autorin ist die einer praktisch orientierten Abteilungsleiterin, zustaending fuer die Planung des Unterrichtsgeschehens, inklusiv Materialerstellung, Fuehrung der Lehrkraefte. Alle Lehrkraefte kommen aus englischsprachigen Laendern.

Schluesselworte: Debattieren, Leadership, Militaerische Fortbildung, Kultur, Argumentation, Oeffentliches Reden

Lernern helfen die Sprachkompetenz Distinguished zu erreichen

James E. Bernhardt, Ph.D. (Foreign Service Institute, emeritiert)

Der vorliegende Artikel macht den Vorschlag, dass eine Aufgabe, die alle Lerner, die die Sprachkompetenz Superior erreicht haben und nun die Kompetenz Distinguished anstreben, gemeinsam haben, ist die Notwendigkeit ihren Wortschatz zu verdoppeln. Es wird weiterhin vorgeschlagen, dass Lernmaterialien fuer die Distinguished Kompetenz massenhaft input enthalten: zum Lesen, Hoeren und Film, TV und internet based Material. Weiterhin werden verschiedene Methoden empfholen, alle wortschatzbezogen, die sicherstellen sollen, dass die Materialien dem Level der Lernenden und deren Bedurfnissen, Lernzielen und Interessen entsprechen.

Der Artikel nimmt high-level Lernprogramme ins Visier und merkt an, dass nicht alle Lernenden in einem Programm zum Level Distinguished dieselben Endziele haben. Auf diesem Level aendern sich die Lernziele von Lerner zu Lerner.

Ihre Lernziele und die Bedurfnisse der Organisationen, die diese Fortbildung finanzieren, sind gewiss anders als es ACTFL Standards und die ILR Kompetenzbeschreibungen andeuten: Beredsamkeit, Mitgliedschaft in einer exklusiven Gruppe der hochgebildeten Elite, und die Faehigkeit fast druckreif reden zu koennen.

Der Artikel behauptet, dass Studenten Rechte haben, die, wenn sie wahrgenommen werden, die Richtung eines Lehrgangs aendern koennen, auch noch in der Mitte eines Kurses. Im weiteren werden Wege zum Erfolg untersucht. Blooms Taxonomie wird abgelehnt, die Benutzung von einer kognitiven Ausrichtung von Lernprogrammen wird vorgeschagen mit einem besonderen Schwerpunkt auf Woertern, Wortfamilien, und die Wichtigkeit des Ausmasses des Wortschatzes der Lernenden zu wissen und deren Lesegeschwindigkeit.

Wenn Lehrkraefte ihre Lerner gut kennen, koennen sie mit den Lernern und Stakeholders fuer jeden Lernenden einen Lernplan entwickeln der ihren genauen Bedurfnissen entgegenkommt.

Schluesselwoerter: Wortschatz, Lernziele, Rechte, Blooms Taxonomie, Text Profilierung

Roadmaps zum Erlangen der Sprechkompetenz Distinguished

Jack Franke (Defense Language Institute Foreign Language Center)

Obwohl das Studium im Ausland in den Vereinigten Staaten als sine qua non fuer den Erwerb der Distinguished Kompetenz gilt, so ist das Auslandsstudium kein Allerheilsmittel dafuer. Diese Studie versucht, herauszufinden, inwieweit Beharrlichkeit, Hartnaeckigkeit, Studium im Ausland, Motivation und Lerner Autonomie zusammenspielen um den Distinguished Level zu erreichen. Mit Hilfe des theoretischen Rahmens der Komplexitaetstheorie und eines phaenomenologischen Designs benutzt diese Studie Interviews mit vier Lehrkraeften an einem Institut in den westlichen Vereinigten Staaten als Hauptquellen der Datensammlung. Diese Studie untersuchte die roadmaps, die erfolgreiche Sprachlehrkraefte benutzt haben, um das Ziel Distinguished Sprechkompetenz zu erreichen durch Interviews und Dokumentarforschung. Die Datenauswertung der Interviews mit den Teilnehmern ergab, dass der Erwerb der Distinguished Sprechkompetenz ein hoechst persoeliches Unterfangen ist. Diese Anstrengungen waren durchweg gekennzeichnet von verschiedenen Motivationen je nach Wahl der Sprache, Engagement in der Zielkultur, Hartnaeckigkeit und Zeit. Zusammenfassend waren die Teilnehmer effektive Selbst-Lerner. Viele waren mit Sprechern der Zielsprache verheiratet und verbrachten geraume Zeit in der fremden Kultur und Gemeinde. Die Studie zeigt moegliche roadmaps fuer Lerner, die die Sprechkompetemz Distinguished erreichen moechten, dem Level der fast Muttersprachlerin.

Schluesselwoerter: Hartnaeckigkeit, Beharrllichkeit, Ausland Studium, Motovierung, Lerner Autonomie, Distinguished Sprechkompetenz

An der Grenze: Matrizen zur Durchfuehrung formativer Auswertungen unter Einbeziehung der Zone proximaler Entwicklung

Betty Lou Leaver Ph.D. (MSI Press)

Die Schlucht zwischen den verschiedenen Levels der Sprachkompetenz (ILR -1,-2-,3, -4/ACTFL Novice, Intermediate, Advanced, Distinguished) ist riesig. Diese Kluft zu ueberqueren kann vieleJahre in Anspruch nehmen-bis zu 17 Jahre fuer Level4 Sprachbenutzer. Die Grenzmatrizen, die unter der Schirmherrschaft des National Foreign Language Centers entwickelt wurden mit vielen L-4 Nutzern, konzentrieren sich auf die Kompetenz Elemente, die notwendig sind um von einer Leistungsstufe zur anderen zu gelangen und dieses Wissen nutzen mit formativen Beurteilungen, um zu entscheiden, welche naechsten Schritte fuer den einzelnen Lerner zu treffen sind auf Grundlage der jeweiligen zone of proximal development. Die Matrizen sind fuer Englisch, Franzoesisch, Russisch, und Spanisch vorhanden und koennen als Vorlagen fuer andere Sprachen genutzt werden.

Schluesselwoerter: Kompetenzgrenzen, Grenz Matrizen, zone of proximal development, formative Beurteilung, Kompetenz Levels

Protokoll zentrierte formative Beurteilung: Evolution und Revolution am Dense Language Institute Foreign Language Center (DLIFLC)

Andrew R. Corin, Ph.D. (DLIFLC, emeritus) & Sergey Entis (DLIFLC, retired)

Protokoll zentrierte formative Beurteilung (PBFA) kann ein starkes Werkzeug sein zur Verbesserung des Lernens und der Diagnostizierung von Lernherausforderungen. Doch es gibt eine inhaerente Spannung zwischen Wirksamkeit und Effiziens bei der Durchfuehrung von PBFAD. Das kann durch viele strategische Massnahmen anggegangen werden: PBFAD Rationierung auf einzelne Faelle von Lernschwierigkeiten; PBFA mit allen Lernenden durchfuehren aber in weniger Faellen, groessere Effiziens in den PBFA selbst einbauen. Egal welche Strategie gewaehlt wird, es wird angenommen, dass PBFA integraler Bestandteil des taeglichen Unterrichtsgeschehens ist und bleibt.

Dieser Artikel beschreibt das Dilemma, wie es sich von 1989 bis 2015 am DLIFLC gestaltet hat und die Massnahmen, die getroffen wurden um PBFA zu erhalten.

Schluesselwoerter: diagnostische/formative/dynamische Beurteilung, Zone der proximalen Entwicklung, Lerner Variablen, Lernstile, Text Typologie, Sprachkompetenz, Weltsprachen Unterricht, Fremdsprachenunterricht; Defense Language Institute Foreign Language Center

Abstracts in Russian

Irene Krasner

Поверх языка: дебаты как высокоинтенсивное средство развития культурного взаимодействия и лидерства

Эмили Клере (Французский Военный Колледж)

В этой статье обсуждается использование дебатов в высшем профессиональном военном образовании, в частности в парижском Французском Военном Колледже с целью помочь офицерам овладеть английским языком на уровне родного.

Во Франции высшее профессиональное военное образование (ВПВО) предоставлено двумя школами - Ecole de Guerre (Французский Военный Колледж) и Centre des hautes études militaires (Центр Высших Военных Исследований). Пример, который исследуется в этой статье, — это использование дебатов кафедрой английского языка для создания условий для офицеров для достижения уровня владения носителей языка за время их годичного курса во Французском Военном Колледже. Точка зрения автора — это точка зрения практикующего преподавателя, который возглавляет этот отдел, разрабатывает курсы, руководит преподавательским составом и преподает. Все преподаватели отдела родом из англоязычных стран.

Ключевые слова: дебаты, лидерство, (французское) военное образование, культура, аргументация, публичные выступления.

Помощь учащимся в достижении высоко продвинутого уровня владения языком Джеймс Э. Бернхардт, доктор философии. (Институт Дипломатии, в отставке)

В настоящей статье утверждается, что основная задача всех учащихся, достигших продвинутого уровня владения языком и желающих достичь высоко продвинутого уровня, заключается в необходимости удвоить размер их словарного запаса. В статье предлагаются планы для обучения на высоко продвинутом уровне, которые включают большое количество входных данных посредством чтения, прослушивания и просмотра видео материалов. Статья также рассматривает ряд способов, основанных на анализе словарного запаса, для оценки того, соответствуют ли материалы уровню учащихся, и аргументирует в пользу материалов, которые соответствуют потребностям, целям и интересам отдельных учащихся.

В статье подробно рассматриваются цели программ более высокого уровня и отмечается, что не все учащиеся, работающие над достижением высоко продвинутого уровня владения языком, имеют в виду одни и те же конечные цели. Их цели на этом уровне различаются от одного учащегося к другому. Цели и потребности организаций, которые финансируют их обучение, также, безусловно, отличаются от определений высоко продвинутого уровня квалификации, соответствующего стандартам ACTFL и описаниям уровней языка ILR: беглость речи, принадлежность к узкому кругу высоко образованных и умение говорить сходное с письменной речью.

В статье утверждается, что у студентов есть свобода выбора, которая при ее осуществлении может изменить траекторию каждого курса даже посередине. Статья исследует пути, ведущие к успеху студентов, отказываясь от использования таксономии Блума и предлагая использовать дизайн-мышление для создания учебной программы. В статье уделяется внимание методам оценки пригодности материалов для обучения, при этом особое внимание уделяется словарю, семействам слов, а также важности знания размера словарного запаса учащегося и скорости, с которой он читает.

Если преподаватели хорошо знают своих учеников, они могут, работая с учащимися и другими заинтересованными лицами создать план обучения для каждого учащегося, который точно соответствует его потребностям.

Ключевые слова: лексика, цели, права, таксономия Блума, профилирование текста.

Планирование, приводящее к высоко продвинутому уровню владения разговорным языком

|Джэк Франке (Центр иностранных языков института обороны)

Несмотря на то, что обучение за границей рассматривается в Соединенных Штатах как sine qua non, этот опыт не является панацеей для достижения высоко продвинутого уровня владения иностранным языком. В данном исследовании делается попытка выяснить, как настойчивость, обучение за границей, мотивация и самостоятельность/автономия учащегося влияют на достижение выдающихся навыков владения разговорной речи. Используя как основу теорию сложности и феноменологический дизайн, исследование в качестве основного инструмента сбора данных использует интервью с четырьмя преподавателями одного из западных институтов Соединенных Штатов. В данном исследовании с помощью интервью и документальных данных изучается планирование, которое успешные преподаватели иностранных языков использовали для достижения выдающихся навыков разговорной речи их студентами. Анализ данных интервью с участниками показал, что высоко продвинутый уровень владения речью был основан на глубоко личном стремлении студента, характеризующимся различными мотивами, основанными на выборе иностранного языка, вовлеченности в его культуру, упорстве и времени. В целом, участники были предельно самодостаточны, многие из них были женаты или замужем за носителями языка и провели длительное время в их культуре и обществе. Это исследование обрисовывает возможные сценарии планирования обучения для преподавателей и студентов, которые хотят добиться уровня владения иностранным языком близкого к носителю этого языка.

Ключевые слова: настойчивость, обучение за границей, автономия учащегося, выдающееся владение речью, мотивация.

Пороговые уровни: матрицы формирующего тестирования, включающие рассмотрение зоны ближайшего развития

Бетти Лу Ливер, доктор философии. (ООО «МСИ Пресс»)

Расстояние между различными квалификационными уровнями (ILR -1, -2, -3, 4/ACTFL Novice, Intermediate, Advanced, Distinguished) велика и достижение следующего уровня может занять много лет — до 17 для некоторых уровней, например, 4-ого языкового уровня. Описание пределов каждого уровня, разработанные под эгидой Национального центра иностранных языков при участии большого числа пользователей языка 4-го уровня, сосредоточены на элементах владения языком, критически важных для перехода с одного уровня на другой, и на том, как использовать эти знания в купе с формирующей тестированием для определения наилучшего пути развития каждого учащегося исходя из его зон ближайшего развития. Таблицы, разработанные для английского, французского, русского и испанского языков, можно использовать для разработки аналогичных таблиц других языков.

Ключевые слова: пределы языковых уровней, матрицы пределов уровней, зона ближайшего развития, формирующее тестирование, уровни владения языком.

Формирующее тестирование, основанное на установленных протоколах: эволюция и революция в Институте Иностранных Языков Министерства Обороны

Эндрю Р. Корин, доктор философии (Центр Иностранных Языков Министерства Обороны, в отставке) и Сергей Энтис (Центр Иностранных Языков Министерства Обороны, в отставке)

Формирующее тестирование на основе протоколов (PBFA) может быть мощным инструментом для улучшения обучения и диагностики проблем обучения. Тем не менее, существует существенное противоречие между эффективностью и действенностью в реализации PBFA. Эту проблему можно решить с помощью различных стратегий: «нормирование» PBFA в зависимости от индивидуальных трудностей в обучении; применение PBFA ко всем учащимся, но в меньшем количестве случаев; или за счет повышения эффективности протоколов. Независимо от принятой стратегии считается само собой разумеющимся, что PBFA должен быть максимально интегрирован с формирующим тестированием как неотъемлемый компонент повседневного обучения в классе. В этой статье описывается дилемма, возникшая в Центре Иностранных Языков Министерства Обороны (DLIFLC) в период с 1989 по 2015 год, и стратегия, которая была принята для преодоления трудностей путем изменения дизайна PBFA.

Ключевые слова: диагностическая оценка; формирующее тестирование; динамическая тестирование; зона ближайшего развития; переменные данные учащегося; стили обучения; типология текста; владение языком; образование на основе мировых языков; изучение иностранного языка; Центр Иностранных Языков Министерства Обороны

Abstracts in Spanish

Tanya de Hoyos

Más allá del lenguaje. Debate del compromiso cultural y de alta intensidad y liderazgo

Emilie Cleret (French War College, París)

Este artículo analiza el uso del debate en la enseñanza militar profesional (PME, por sus siglas en inglés) en la Escuela de Guerra (French War College) de París para ayudar a los oficiales a alcanzar un nivel de competencia lingüística en inglés similar a la de un nativo. En Francia, la Enseñanza Militar Profesional superior (PME) se imparte en dos escuelas: la Escuela de Guerra y el Centro para Estudios Militares Superior (French War College y Centre for Higher Military Studies). Este artículo analiza el uso del debate en el Departamento de Estudios Ingleses para apoyar el esfuerzo de los oficiales y alcanzar un nivel de competencia lengua extranjera, similar a un nativo durante su curso de un año en la Escuela de Guerra Francesa (French War College). La perspectiva del autor es que un practicante dirija este departamento, diseñe los cursos y administre al personal docente. Todos los miembros del profesorado deben ser de países anglófonos.

Palabras clave: Debate, liderazgo, enseñanza militar (francesa), cultura, argumentación, oratoria

Apoyo para que los alumnos alcancen un nivel de competencia magisterial

James E. Bernhardt, Ph.D. (Doctor emérito del Foreign Service Institute)

El presente artículo propone que la tarea que deben tener en común todos los alumnos que han alcanzado niveles superiores de competencia y desean alcanzar el nivel distinguido es la necesidad de duplicar el vocabulario adquirido. El artículo sugiere que los diseños educativos para la formación de nivel magisterial deberán incluir cantidades masivas de lectura, audio comprensión y observación. También propone una serie de métodos basados en vocabulario para evaluar si los materiales se ajustan al nivel de los alumnos, y si los materiales se adaptan a las necesidades, objetivos e intereses de cada alumno en particular.

El texto examina, detenidamente, los objetivos de los programas de nivel superior y señala que no todos los estudiantes que trabajan para alcanzar niveles distinguidos de competencia tienen en mente los mismos objetivos finales. Sus metas, a este nivel, difieren de un alumno a otro. Sus objetivos y las necesidades de las organizaciones que pagan, por el entrenamiento, tienen características distintas del nivel de proficiencia distinguida de acuerdo con las normas establecidas por ACTFL y en las descripciones de los niveles de destreza del ILR: elocuencia, pertenencia a un grupo selecto de estudiantes educados y la capacidad para hablar, de manera aproximada, como los textos escritos a nivel académico.

El escrito afirma que los estudiantes tienen un conjunto de derechos que, cuando se ejercen, pueden cambiar la trayectoria de cada curso, incluso a mitad del camino. También el escrito examina diferentes caminos para alcanzar el éxito, rechaza el uso de la taxonomía de Bloom y sugiere el uso de enfoques de pensamiento de diseño para engrandecer el programa de instrucción. Se presta atención a las técnicas para evaluar el profesionalismo de los materiales para el entrenamiento, con enfoque especial en vocabulario, grupos de palabras y la importancia de que el estudiante tenga un amplio banco de palabras y pueda leerlas rápidamente. Cuando los instructores conocen bien a sus alumnos, pueden en colaboración con ellos y las partes interesadas, crear un plan de aprendizaje para que cada alumno satisfaga sus necesidades específicas.

Palabras clave: Vocabulario, objetivos, derechos, taxonomía de Bloom, perfil del texto

Hojas de ruta para el dominio de producción oral distinguido

Jack Franke (Defense Language Institute Foreign Language Center)

Aunque los estudios en el extranjero se consideran en Estados Unidos una condición sine qua non, la experiencia de estudiar en el extranjero no es una panacea para lograr una competencia lingüística distinguida. Este estudio intenta descubrir cómo la persistencia, los estudios en el extranjero, la motivación y la autonomía del estudiante influyen en la consecución de una competencia oral distinguida. El proyecto se apoya en el marco teórico de la teoría de la complejidad y el diseño fenomenológico y utilizó entrevistas de cuatro educadores del instituto Western United States como principal instrumento de la recolección de datos. Este estudio investigó las hojas de ruta de los educadores que han tenido estudiantes que han logrado tener competencia oral distinguida mediante entrevistas e investigación documentada. El análisis de los datos de las entrevistas con los participantes reveló que la competencia oral distinguida era una búsqueda muy personal, caracterizada por diferentes motivos basados en la elección de una lengua extranjera, el compromiso con la cultura de destino, la valoración y el tiempo. En general, los participantes fueron estudiantes muy conscientes de sí mismos, muchos estaban casados con personas de habla extranjera e invirtieron mucho tiempo en la cultura y la comunidad para mejorar sus habilidades lingüísticas. El estudio proporcionó posibles hojas de ruta para estudiantes y educadores que deseaban alcanzar un dominio casi nativo de una lengua extranjera.

Palabras clave: Persistencia, estudios en el extranjero, motivación, autonomía del alumno, dominio distinguido del idioma

En la cúspide: Estructuras para orientar la evaluación formativa incorporando la consideración de la zona de desarrollo próximo

Betty Lou Leaver, Ph.D. (MSI Press LLC)

El abismo que separa los distintos niveles de competencia (ILR: 1, 2, 3, 4/ACTFL Novato, Intermedio, Avanzado y Distinguido) es tan amplio que atravesar el espacio entre los niveles puede tomar muchos años, hasta 17, en el caso de algunos estudiantes de idiomas de nivel 4. Las Cuadrículas Cúspides (Cusp Grids), desarrolladas por el National Foreign Language Center con
la colaboración de un gran número de usuarios de nivel 4, se centran en elementos de competencia críticos para pasar de un nivel a otro y en cómo utilizar este conocimiento con la evaluación formativa para determinar los mejores pasos a seguir para cada estudiante, basándose en sus zonas de desarrollo próximo. Las cuadrículas que se ofrecen para inglés, francés, ruso y español pueden servir de guía para elaborar cuadrículas similares en otros idiomas.

Palabras clave: Cúspides de competencia, cuadrículas de cúspides, zona de desarrollo próximo, evaluación formativa, niveles de competencia

Evaluación formativa basada en protocolos: Evolución y revolución en el Defense Language Institute

Andrew R. Corin, Ph. D. (Defense Language Institute Foreign Language Center, emeritus) y Sergey Entis (Defense Language Institute Foreign Language Center, retirado)

La evaluación formativa basada en protocolos (PBFA, por sus siglas en inglés) puede ser una herramienta poderosa para mejorar el aprendizaje y diagnosticar los problemas de aprendizaje. Sin embargo, existe una tensión inherente entre la eficacia y la eficiencia en la aplicación del PBFA. Esto puede abordarse mediante diversas estrategias: "racionar;" el PBFA para casos de estudiantes con dificultades individuales de aprendizaje; utilizar el PBFA con todos los estudiantes, pero en casos especiales o mediante la ingeniería de una mayor eficiencia del protocolo. Independientemente de la estrategia adoptada, se da por sentado que el PBFA debe integrarse al máximo con la evaluación formativa basada en la instrucción (IBFA, por sus siglas en inglés), como componente integral de la instrucción diaria en el aula. Este artículo se apoyó en el dilema que se llevó a cabo en el Defense Language Institute Foreign Language Center (DLIFLC, por sus siglas en inglés) entre 1989 y 2015 y el camino seguido para superarlo mediante el rediseño del PBFA.

Palabras clave: Evaluación diagnóstica; evaluación formativa; evaluación dinámica; zona de desarrollo próximo; variables del alumno; estilos de aprendizaje; tipología textual; competencia lingüística; educación lenguas del mundo, enseñanza de lenguas extranjeras; Defense Language Institute Foreign Language Center

BOOK REVIEWS

Lessons from Exceptional Language Learners
Who Have Achieved Nativelike Proficiency:
Motivation, Cognition, and Identity

Authors: **Zoltan Dörnyei and Katarine Mentzelopoulos**
Publisher: **Multilingual Matters 2022**

Summary

This book analyzes the findings of a research project that Zoltan Dörnyei, a prolific and esteemed contributor to the field of language learning, designed for his students at the University of Nottingham when his course, the *Psychology of Bilingualism and Language Learning*, moved online. This is unfortunately a posthumous publication, for Zoltan Dörnyei passed away earlier this fall. His co-author, Katarina Mentzelopoulos, opens the volume by sharing her memories of working with him.

Dörnyei had asked his students to identify second language (L2) learning success stories, adult learners who managed to achieve nativelike L2 proficiency studying their L2 after puberty and without extensive experience in an L2 environment earlier. These champions of language learning often pass as native speakers with interlocutors conversing in their native language. They can blend in fully. His students found thirty such elite language learners whose learning paths are described in the companion volume, *Stories from Exceptional Language Learners Who Have Achieved Native like Proficiency*. As a group they did not take aptitude or proficiency tests.

This volume represents an in-depth, qualitative research report following academic conventions, while the companion publication presents the unique life narratives of those thirty individuals who arrived at native like L2 proficiency.

Evaluation

Both volumes are of interest to anyone interested in the process of language learning: in teaching, counseling, or seeking to improve an already very high level of L2. The stories are irresistible, and an examination of chapter topics reveals attention to such important topics as: forging an L2 identity, sources of persistence, attention to pronunciation, intensive effort and strategic learning, cognition and other facilitative learner characteristics, and a unique bond with the chosen language, to name a few. While a review of the literature on exceptional language learners is presented in the first chapter, every chapter includes references to previous studies that are relevant to what is being discussed in that chapter. There are eleven pages of reference works that are used effectively throughout the volume to help place these learners' experiences and insights into the continuum of exploring L2 learning at the highest levels of achievement. In discussing learning strategies, for example:

"What emerges from the existing reviews (Bierdon & Pawlak, 2016: Hyltenstam et al., 2018; Leaver & Campbell, 2014; Moyer, 2021) is that native like and near-native like learners adopt highly personalized learning strategies and are, in fact, often largely self-taught."(p. 7)

Canadian participant Kristopher is a case in point. He started studying Mandarin in high school after a very negative experience with French in grade school. Kristopher met a Chinese family and asked if he could visit them. Every day after school he just sat with them in their living room, listening. He started to learn Japanese at the age of 22 while living in the country. There he visited a local pub to just sit and listen to everyone around him. He didn't speak to others in the early stages of his language learning. He is currently a professor of Japanese literature in Japan. He is taken for a native speaker (when his interlocutors are not able to see him) in both Mandarin and Japanese.

For Kristopher, as well as for many of the other participants, the role of pronunciation was of paramount importance. An entire chapter is devoted to this sub-skill. Kristopher strove to get each tone exactly right. He also sang Japanese folk songs with a group. Timur, from Kazakhstan, worked on his English with linguistic programs and was thus able to identify that his initial "T" sounds needed to be aspirated. Joy, a Canadian living in Iceland, strove to sound like her husband. She was both musical, regularly singing in church, and a good mimic. Others referred to mimicking their interlocutors, whether consciously or unconsciously. For many, music played an important role in their L2 and they identified as being musically inclined, but at least 10% of the participants called attention to their being musically challenged.

The authors wonder whether current trends that pay only cursory attention to pronunciation in foreign language (FL) education haven't impeded some highly successful FL learners from crossing over into the group studied here. They suggest that FL learners can perhaps turn to the acting profession for inspiration and guidance. Actor Amy Walker has a YouTube channel focused on accents and a coaching practice, for example. Actors wishing to audition for a wider variety of roles work on specific accents to depict a character they might not normally play. Conquering the accent allows them to enter a new world, just as the participants of this study were able to fully enter their L2 identities.

Previous studies of very advanced students have focused primarily on educated adult learners in professional training programs of various types (Leaver, Ehrman & Shekhtman, 2005 and Leaver, 2003). There has been a prescriptive element in evidence suggesting many possible ways to enrich the program and the instruction, as well as the self- efficacy of the learner.

This study, however, provides no such practical suggestions. The group studied here is younger. Two participants are 16 and four others are in their 20s. Many are immigrants and their educational backgrounds vary considerably. This study may not be particularly relevant for academic FL teaching and learning. It could, however, be very useful for all those working with immigrant FL programs in high school and community college. It could also benefit student counselors and students themselves who may need to be inspired by those who overcame various obstacles to achieving nativelike proficiency. The ability to become linguistically indistinguishable from one's peer group is profoundly significant and life-changing for an immigrant. The current study begins to explore this. It is a good start and there is much more to be learned.

About the Reviewer

Natalia Lord is a retired Learning Counselor from the Language Consultation Service, School of Language Studies at the Foreign Service Institute. Previously she taught Russian at FSI and co-developed, with Boris Shekhtman, an advanced course aimed at the distinguished level of proficiency. She also taught Russian and Russian Literature at Howard University. Her publications include contributions to two books on teaching methods, as well as a previous JDLS article. She currently teaches courses in Russian Literature for Encore Learning in Arlington, Virginia.

Mastering Italian through Global Debate

Authors: **Marie Bertola and Sandra Carletti**
Publisher: **Georgetown University Press, 2023**

Summary

Mastering Italian Through Global Debate (2022) is divided into six chapters, each one focusing on a different topical subject relevant to the current global debate. The first chapter centers on ecology. It includes a reading exercise and an argumentative essay on plastic and its environmental and economic impact. The second chapter addresses the topic of globalism versus localism, with a focus on the Covid-19 pandemic's effect on both phenomena. In chapter three, the conversation brings attention to the themes of economic inequality, self-sufficiency, and redistribution of wealth. Chapter four takes on immigration, multiculturalism, and diversity, while chapter five addresses the question of security and individual freedom, and the clash between mass surveillance and privacy. Finally, in chapter six, the book discusses STEM and the Arts and Humanities, and the connection among the different disciplines. The book also includes two appendices, which provide directions regarding learning methodologies and assessment and evaluation criteria.

Evaluation

Per the Interagency Language Roundtable (ILR) Scale, a level 4 speaker demonstrates an advanced professional proficiency. This level includes the ability to play an effective role among native speakers in such contexts as conferences, lectures and debates on matters of disagreement to include the ability to advocate a position at length, both formally and in chance encounters, using sophisticated verbal strategies. Through debate, students learn how to make hypotheses, support conclusions with evidence, and deploy rhetoric of persuasion in the target language. *Mastering Italian Through Global Debate* provides structured activities which can be offered in a synchronous online teaching environment or in individual classrooms.

Shekhtman et al. (2003) propose that presentational speech will aid students in acquiring professional vocabulary. Each chapter provides excellent opportunities for vocabulary development introduced as collocations. Once students become familiar with the vocabulary, they then prepare for the debate. Each chapter begins with reading assignments which are meant to activate students' background knowledge. "Background knowledge includes all the experiences that a reader brings to a text: life experiences, educational experiences, knowledge of how texts are organized" (Brown & Brown 2016). The topics proposed in each chapter are rich and stimulating. The authors' objective is, as a result of learning how to debate, gaining knowledge on multiple global current topics which in turn will increase lexical competencies and active listening skills.

From a curricular design perspective, the book adopts an Open Architecture Curricula Design (OACD) approach (Campbell 2021). Some of the characteristics of OACD are the use of authentic materials, project/scenario-based instruction, development and use of higher-order thinking skills, and incorporation of collaborative learning, which we see implemented in all sections of the book. The topics chosen by the authors are stimulating and are typically source of debate in Italy among native speakers. Students are exposed to a series of structured activities comprised of reading assignments, listening assignments, and writing assignments which are all geared toward the final debate on the topics covered. Shekhtman et al. (2003) highlight seven tasks that Level 4 professional language users should be able to accomplish: 1) problem-solving discussion, 2) informally interpreting language and culture, 3) interview, 4) briefing, 5) formal presentation, 6) debate, and 7) negotiation. The authors expertly expose students to all seven tasks through the effective use of role playing, authentic materials, and activities aimed at stimulating higher level thinking skills.

In preparation for the final debate, students are asked to gather all their notes on the topic, key words, collocations, and linguistic structures that can aid in the debate. Students are reminded that they are not allowed to read directly from the notes and can only use them as a reference. This is the culmination of all the preparatory work. At the end of each chapter, students are asked to conduct a self-assessment to include how motivated they were to discuss the topic. This self-assessment is an extremely effective and fundamental final stage in determining language progression because it provides opportunities to reflect on one's own learning process, and it enhances metacognitive skills.

Mastering Italian Through Global Debate is an excellent textbook which can be easily incorporated into an advanced Italian language curriculum because it will aid students and instructors alike in achieving level 4 proficiency.

References

Bertola, M. & Carletti, S. (2022). *Mastering Italian Through Global Debate.* Georgetown University Press.

Campbell, C. (2021). Open Architecture Curricular Design. A fundamental principle of transformative language learning and teaching. In B.L. Leaver, D.E. Davidson, & C. Campbell (Eds.), *Transformative language learning and teaching.* Cambridge, UK: Cambridge University Press.

Interagency Language Roundtable. (2022). Description of Proficiency Levels. Interagency Language Roundtable Downloaded from https://www.govtilr.org/Skills/ILRscale1.htm.

Shekhtman, B., Lord, N., & Kuznetsova, E. (2003). Complication exercises for raising the oral proficiency level of highly advanced language students. *Journal for Distinguished Language Studies 1.*

T. Brown, & J. Brown (2016). *Teaching Advanced Language Skills Through Global Debate: Theory and Practice.* Tony Brown and Jennifer Brown. Georgetown University Press.

About the Reviewers

Alessandra Rice is an Italian native speaker and a former Associate Professor of the Defense Language Institute Foreign Language Center in Monterey, CA, where she taught Italian, Diagnostic Assessment and coordinated study abroad programs. She has also been a language consultant for ACTFL for the past ten years.

Francesca Gasparella is an Italian native speaker who is fluent is fluent in English, French, Spanish, Portuguese, and Arabic. She holds a BA in Languages, Cultures and Societies of the Middle East and North Africa from the Ca' Foscari University of Venice, Italy, and an MA in Middle East and North Africa Studies from the University of Strasbourg, France. A passionate linguist, Francesca has experience teaching ESL and Italian at all levels of proficiency.

Mastering Spanish through Global Debate

Authors: **Nieves Pérez Knapp, Krishuana Hines-Gaither, and Morella Ruscitti-Tovar**

Publisher: **Georgetown University Press 2022**

Summary

The textbook, *Mastering Spanish through Global Debate* (2022), focuses on skill development for advanced Spanish students to reach the competencies of Superior established by the *American Council on the Teaching of Foreign Languages* (ACTFL). The introduction to the book centers on its mission: to foster Superior language expertise in Spanish based on ACTFL proficiency benchmarks and the NCSSFL-ACTFL Can-Do statements. The introduction includes a breakdown of and rationale for each activity type included in every chapter. The book is divided into six chapters and centers on diverse, yet universal, international thematic issues. The six chapters are: 1) The Environment and the Economy: An Economy of Colors, 2) Intervention or Isolation: The Dilemma of Democracy and Interventionism, 3) Redistribution of Wealth or Self-Sufficiency: The Economic Gap---Is a Fair Distribution of Wealth Possible? 4) Cultural Conservation or Diversity: Immigration---Threat or Plurality? 5) National Security or Personal Liberty, and 6) Formal Education or Professional Experience. The appendices include steps for structuring a debate and a rubric to evaluate oral and written work.

Each chapter follows a similar structure with scaffolding and a natural progression of Superior-skill development. A "Before the Reading" section introduces the theme of the chapter with questions and topics related to the issue, linguistic notes and a concept map for students to elaborate on the subject and to organize prior knowledge of the chapter theme. Next, there is a debate activity with short proverbs and quotes. The subsequent section, "Studying the Theme," centers on a focused reading and comprehension questions. Each of these chapter readings present facts, statistics and various sides of the debate in an objective way and provides more in-depth background information about the issue covered in the chapter. Readings include statistics and anecdotes with an emphasis on Latin America but are also global in context with the inclusion of other countries and regions such as China and Scandinavia. After the focused reading, there is a vocabulary section with academic terms for vocabulary expansion. A practice debate follows in which students must role-play opposing or differing positions based on the selected scenarios. Next, a listening comprehension section with questions ensues. A second reading on the topic, an opinion essay, highlights one perspective from the chapter topic and the readers must interpret the viewpoint through the guided questions that follow. The culminating assignments: a persuasive essay of five to six paragraphs, a three to five-minute presentation and a debate conclude the material of each chapter with a brief self-reflection section for the debate and chapter vocabulary at the very end. All chapters also incorporate activities with the *Corpus del espagnole* website, *https://corpusdelespanol.org*, which is an external Spanish online corpus and is free to use with registration.

Evaluation

This text is a needed addition for Spanish programs as many students struggle to reach Superior proficiency benchmarks (Leaver & Shekhtman, 2002). While most upper-division texts, particularly for conversation and writing, focus on the Advanced level, *Mastering Spanish through Global Debate*'s exclusive attention on the Superior level makes the text unique and valuable as a resource or a standalone text. The materials and activities embedded in the text create a structure designed to challenge students through critical thinking, issue and perspective analyses, debates and it exposes them abundantly to academic and scholarly language.

The greatest strength of this textbook is the focus on constant active learning and language production targeted exclusively for the Superior level. The text demands copious language output from students and has high-quality activities and content. The authors have a persistent focus on these competences with ample discussion questions, readings that address Superior-level topics, debates and listening activities. The discussion and debate sections are rich with plentiful thought-provoking questions and scenarios that elicit Superior-level responses. The vocabulary sections guide students to gain Superior-level language terminology. The book structures activities to empower students to use hypotheticals, defend opinions, and speak abstractly on a range of topics. The culminating assignments link new learning and skills to display Superior proficiency based on the chapter theme.

Each chapter thoroughly develops the necessary skills for Superior proficiency: interpersonal communication, presentational speaking, presentational writing, interpretive listening and interpretive reading. The textbook aligns with NCSSFL-ACTFL Can-Do Statements intentionally, consistently and seamlessly. Advanced proficiency in Spanish is assumed and vital to complete the activities in this textbook, as there is little focus on the practice and review of Advanced proficiency levels and Can-Do statements. This textbook expertly addresses the frustration of general upper-division texts that do not focus sufficiently on the Superior level. University Spanish programs could design a standalone course, such as Superior Spanish, in conjunction with this text, as a strategy to target Superior proficiency. The recommended audience for this textbook is students and professionals who have mastered the Advanced skills and who desire to gain the tools to reach Superior. This is a text designed for senior undergraduates, graduate students, and professionals with strong motivation to progress Spanish-language skills. In particular, this text is of tremendous value for students of Spanish studying international studies, international business, geography, political science, and government. As instructional material for a high proficiency level, a course implementing *Mastering Spanish* will require perceptive and quality feedback from seasoned language instructors in order to carry out the learning goals of this textbook effectively---a task that should not be taken lightly.

All textbooks, naturally, have minor limitations. *Mastering Spanish* has very few and none of them affects the impressive contribution of this text. One of the more salient restrictions is that there is limited freedom for student choice in the activities and topics, with some exception in the culminating activities. Because all topics are preordained, the students will have few opportunities to explore topics of their personal or professional interest related to the Superior level that may be beyond the scope of the chapter themes. Additionally, an expanded self-reflection section would add value to the end of each chapter. The website, https://corpusdelespanol.org, has a learning curve that may appear overwhelming at first, but offers valuable and comprehensive data related to each word searched, its collocations, and web sources. Finally, each chapter presents only one Can-Do statement in the introduction. Because this text integrates the Superior Can-Do statements so fully, the authors could make the connection between additional Can-Do statements and the activities of each chapter even more explicit.

Mastering Spanish through Global Debate is a pioneering work and is highly recommended for educators and professionals alike with motivation to tackle the elusive Superior level through teaching and learning Superior language for Spanish with laser precision and focus. The addition of this well-designed and well-researched text to the Spanish-teaching corpus is most welcome and the profession would benefit from additional texts that address Superior language skills in such detail.

References

ACTFL Proficiency Guidelines 2012. Downloaded from https://www.actfl.org/sites/default/files/guidelines/ACTFLProficiencyGuidelines2012.pdf

Corpus del español. https://corpusdelespanol.org

Interagency Language Roundtable. (2022). Description of Proficiency Levels. Interagency Language Roundtable Downloaded from https://www.govtilr.org/Skills/ILRscale1.htm.

Knapp, N.P., K. Hines-Gaither, M. Ruscitti-Tovar. (2022). *Mastering Spanish through Global Debate.* Georgetown University Press.

Leaver, B. L., & Shekhtman, B. (2002). Principles and practices in teaching Superior-level language skills: Not just more of the same. In B. L. Leaver & B. Shekhtman (Eds.), *Developing professional-level language proficiency* (pp. 3-33). New York: Cambridge University Press.

NCSSFL-ACTFL Can-Do Statements Proficiency Benchmarks. Downloaded from https://www.actfl.org/sites/default/files/can-dos/Superior%20Distinguished%20Can-Do_Statements.pdf.

About the Reviewer

Joseph Fees, PhD, is an Associate Professor of Spanish and the Online Coordinator for the College of Humanities, Education, and Social Sciences at Delaware State University. His current research interests include language acquisition, faculty training, and program development. In 2021, he won Delaware State University's annual Faculty Excellence in Teaching award, and he has received grants for language program development and language research from ACTFL and the U.S. Department of Education.

Practices That Work: Bringing Learners to Professional Proficiency in World Languages

Editor: **Thomas Jesús Garza**
Publisher: **MSI Press, 2021**

Summary of the book's purpose and contents

Practices That Work: Bring Learners to Professional Proficiency in World Languages, edited by Thomas Jesús Garza, was published in 2021 as an updated and expanded version of the book, *What Works: Helping Students Reach Native-Like Second-Language Competence*, published in 2008. The new edition aims to achieve three main objectives: "1) to show that bringing learners to professional proficiency in world languages in U.S. program *could* be done; 2) to show *how* these results could be attained; and 3) to demonstrate *why* world language education must be part of every educational curriculum and part of every U.S. citizen's consciousness" (Garza, 2021, p. vii). The addition of the third purpose is a notable feature of the revised book. The intended audience is language practitioners seeking new or additional ways to enhance their courses with proven strategies for learner success (Garza, 2021).

Divided into five sections, the book delves into various aspects of language instruction and assessment, providing valuable insights and practical strategies for language educators. Section I: *Focuses on the Learner*, contains seven articles, and offers experiences on learner-centered practices that can improve language proficiency. Leaver (2021) stated that "the evidence is also clear that what works in English as a Second Language may be less effective in Arabic, Chinese, French, German, or Russian as a Second Language" (p. 2). For those who have learned a couple of languages, this is a shared experience and an important one. Different models, approaches, methods, techniques, and strategies need to be adapted or developed for different learners of different world languages. Leaver and Ehrman (2021) declared that "learners must learn to style-flex if they want to achieve native-like proficiency" and offer their observation that "The wise teacher, then, not only adapts lesson plans to learner learning styles but also teaches learning strategies associated with the opposing learning styles and creates activities which require the learner to style-flex on an increasingly frequent basis" (p. 7). Reflective practitioners would agree to that. Being style-flexible is one of the most important strategies a language learner should have because language learners can adapt themselves to different world language learning settings. In Section II: *Focus on Instruction*, eleven articles showcase successful classroom practices that have resulted in significant proficiency gains for near native-like proficiency level students. Shekhtman (2021) encourages the use of models and native speakers rather than dictionaries because they yield much better learning results. This doesn't mean that dictionaries are not important but suggests a more lively and more interactive method of learning a world language. Martin (2021) quoted a Russian expression that "Repetition is the mother of learning!" (p.43). It echoes what Thorndike (1898) proposed in his Law of Exercise which stated that the more times a response is made in a given situation, the stronger it becomes. Section III, *Focus on the Instructor* explores how reflective practitioners play a crucial role in helping students enhance their strategic competence, develop automaticity, and select appropriate teaching methods. Section IV, titled *Focus on Skills*, demonstrates different teaching strategies and methods employed by instructors to improve proficiency gains for superior-level language learners. The authors examine the challenges associated with understanding dialects, highlighting their significance in achieving near native-like proficiency. Kubler (2021) observed that "The importance and difficulty of understanding dialects are reflected in the Interagency Language Roundtable (ILR) Language Skill Level Descriptions, where there is a gradual progression from (at levels 3 and below) no comprehension of dialects; to (at levels 3+ and 4) comprehension of the essentials of speech in some major dialects; to (at levels 4+ and 5) full comprehension of all speech that would be intelligible to a well-educated native speaker, even in a number of 'regional' and 'illiterate' or 'extreme' dialects" (p.81). Most readers, if they are not in the field of learning English to near native-like proficiency, would not notice the Interagency Language Roundtable (ILR)' Language Skill Level Description. Learning dialects of a world language elevates language learning to a whole new level and is most probably one of the most difficult parts of reaching the near nativelike proficiency level. Lastly, Section V: *Focus on Assessment* features three articles that present various models and methods for assessing and evaluating language learning outcomes. These articles provide practical insights and successful practices used by reflective instructors in their classrooms.

Evaluation

This book is the groundbreaking work of Dr. Betty Lou Leaver and other impactful contributors in the field of learning world languages to near native-like proficiency. The authors of the 39 articles in this book strive to offer readers a wide range of proven and successful classroom practices. The primary objectives of this book, as stated by the editor, are twofold: to demonstrate that attaining professional proficiency in world language in the U.S. programs is feasible, and to provide a roadmap for achieving such outcomes. While these goals are well-addressed throughout the book, the addition of the third purpose in the revised edition, "to demonstrate *why* world language education must be part of every educational curriculum and part of every U.S. citizen's consciousness" (Garza, 2021, p.vii), could benefit from further clarity. The importance of world language, especially at the professional proficiency level, is hinted at, but a dedicated section highlighting its significance would enhance the understanding for readers outside of Language Flagship Programs and university settings.

Overall, the articles in this book showcase tangible ways to improve outcomes for superior-level language proficiency students across diverse settings and languages. These practical examples are drawn from real classroom experiences, rigorously tested within Language Flagship Programs and universities. The insights offered by the authors extend beyond the academic sphere, providing valuable suggestions for language practitioners in government and post-secondary institutions.

Throughout the book, the authors draw on extensive research and provide compelling arguments backed by scholarly references. The chapters are well-structured and easy to read, offering clear and concise explanations of concepts and methodologies. Additionally, the inclusion of real-life examples and experiences from language practitioners enhances the book's practicality and relevance.

Undoubtedly, *Practices That Work* has made a significant contribution to the field of world language learning. This book is a valuable resource for language practitioners seeking to enhance their teaching methods and attain superior-level proficiency outcomes, as well as those working with learners at lower proficiency levels. Its practical insights and well-tested methodologies guarantee its relevance and applicability in diverse language learning contexts. With its wealth of insights and field-tested strategies, this book serves as an essential guide for language educators dedicated to nurturing professional language proficiency in their students.

References

Garza, E. J. (Ed.). (2021). *Practices that work: Bringing learners to professional proficiency in world languages.* N/A.

Kubler, C. (2021). Teach dialects. In T. J. Garza (Ed.), *Practices that work: Bringing learners to professional proficiency in world languages* (pp.81-84). N/A.

Leaver, B. L. (2021). Individualize the learning plan. In T. J. Garza (Ed.), *Practices that work: Bringing learners to professional proficiency in world languages* (pp.1-5). N/A.

Leaver, B. L., and Ehrman, M. (2021). Be sensitive to learning styles. In T. J. Garza (Ed.), *Practices that work: Bringing learners to professional proficiency in world languages* (pp.6-8). N/A.

Martin, C. (2021). The importance of models, the power of imitation. In T. J. Garza (Ed.), *Practices that work: Bringing learners to professional proficiency in world languages* (pp.41-43). N/A.

Shekhtman, B. (2021). Encourage the use of models and native speakers rather than dictionaries. In T. J. Garza (Ed.), *Practices that work: Bringing learners to professional proficiency in world languages* (pp.29-30). N/A.

Thorndike, E. L. (1898). Animal intelligence: An experimental study of the associative processes in animals. *The Psychological Review: Monograph Supplements, 2*(4), i–109. https://doi.org/10.1037/h0092987

About the Reviewer

Michael Wei, Ph.D. is Professor and TESOL Program Director, University of Missouri – Kansas City. His research interests include applied linguistics and second language acquisition. He co-edited the book, *Applied Linguistics for Teachers of Culturally and Linguistically Diverse Learners* published by the IGI Global in 2019 and co-authored the book, *The Lived Experience of Chinese International Students in America – An Academic Journey* published by Springer in 2021. He is the 2019 recipient of the UMKC Chancellor's

Award for Excellence in Teaching and the UMKC's 2020 recipient of the Governor's Award for Excellence in Teaching.

Stories from Exceptional Language Learners Who Have Achieved Nativelike Proficiency

Authors: **Katarina Mentzelopoulos and Zoltán Dörnyei with Capucine Trotignon**
Publisher: **Multilingual Matters, 2023, 188 pages**

Since the beginning of the proficiency movement in the 1980s and the alignment of language learning with descriptors of functional ability in the language being studied, nativelike ability became the elusive "gold standard" of success in language learning. While too many learners of a world language find themselves finishing high school or even a university language course with no more than an intermediate level of functional proficiency, the past two decades of research and implementation have demonstrated that intensive methods of instruction, hybrid programs, and other methods of saturating the learning with input while attending to individual differences and learner identities can result in the attainment of ACTFL Superior or even Distinguished (ILR 3 and 4) proficiency.

This volume is appropriately titled, as it tells the stories of thirty diverse learners who, for various motivations and through varied pathways, somehow managed to attain nativelike proficiency in their respective world languages. It is their personal narratives, skillfully collected and redacted from hours of interview data, that drive the volume. The individual stories reflect the experiences of learners aged sixteen to sixty-seven years, representing speakers of sixteen home languages from eighteen countries, and nine target languages of study in which they became exceptionally proficient. While the majority of the languages learned fall into the category of commonly taught (English, German, French), some are less-commonly taught languages: Mandarin, Japanese, Hungarian, Icelandic, and Norwegian.

The learner narratives are divided into seven chapters, each identifying particular characteristics of learner success in attaining nativelike language proficiency. The authors' identification of these personality categories or "journeys" (p. xvii) is both convenient as a device to group the interview participants and reveals the breadth of pathways available to attain high-level proficiency. While some of these characteristics can, of course, overlap and intersect, each chapter presents narratives of individuals for whom one of these traits emerged as dominant in their language learning journey.

Three of the chapters provide interview data to support several notions of conventional wisdom connected to successful language learning. Chapter 3: "A New Generation," for example, presents four cases of success among several of the younger participants in the study, reinforcing the long-held notion that language learning is best achieved in a naturalistic way at younger ages and adding the more recent assertion that facility with new technologies and media may aid the effort to acquire languages, suggesting that members of Gen Z may prove to be the most proficient cohort of language learners to date. In a similar vein, Chapter 4: "An Ear for Languages" offers five stories that support the idea that some individuals possess a more acute sense of listening/hearing to distinguish and imitate sounds and, thus, are more able to discern and produce those of a new idiom. These stories also interrogate the notion that pronunciation plays a relatively small part in overall language proficiency. Finally, the volume's last chapter, Chapter 7: "Success Breeds Success," presents the stories of five learners, all of whom already attained proficiency in another world language(s) and had survived the process to emerge more prepared to take on yet another language and attain the level of nativelike proficiency.

The first two chapters of the volume emphasize particular relationships that individual learners have or have developed regarding the language and culture being learned. In Chapter 1: "A Unique Bond," four learners develop and demonstrate unusually close ties to their respective languages that go beyond the usual "liking" of it and the culture, instead developing a much more affective personal connection with the language. Learners that share this "unique bond" with their respective languages of study are often successful in their pursuit of high-level proficiency. The learners described in Chapter 2: "Escaping the Everyday" also go beyond liking the language that they are learning, but for them acquisition of a new language and culture also signifies their engagement in a new adventure or journey. For these four learners, the new language presented them the opportunity to travel – actually or vicariously – to new parts of the world. In both chapters, the portraits of the individual learners go well beyond the reflexive or impressionistic descriptions that often limit conversations regarding affective features of learning; instead, they offer new and personal ways of understanding these factors in contexts and environments of language learning that helps both learner and instructor better understand the path(s) to advanced proficiencies.

Of particular interest in the current period of attention to diversity and inclusivity in education is the group learner narratives are Chapter 5: "The Desire to Blend In," and Chapter 6: "Shifting Identities." This poignant and sometimes provocative collection of narratives demonstrates how language can play a critical role in determining how an individual's success in language learning may be influenced by identity and self-presentation. Chapter 5: "The Desire to Blend In," presents the stories of four successful learner who all, in one way or another, chose to "to go local" in their quest for proficiency and acceptance in the respective language community. These stories raise numerous questions and issues connected with identity, indigeneity, and belonging that are germane to all language learners and instructors, especially at higher levels of proficiency. In Chapter 6: "Shifting Identities" the learners in this section must contend with issues surrounding a perception of increased importance or acceptance that comes with mastery of a so-called "prestige" language in their home country or environment. From instrumental desires to succeed to more representative expression of gender identity linguistically, this chapter offers four personal accounts of how nativelike mastery of another language helped them more fully express their identities. Reactions such as those Shinhye received from her peers succinctly encapsulate the paradox of the positionality of "going local": "You're a Korean, so *act like a Korean* (italics mine TJG)" (p. 141). What precisely this utterance means for the learner--not to mention for those who said it--is at the core both of attaining nativelike proficiency, as well as of presentation of one's identity in one's own culture.

Among the volume's many strengths, the details of each learner's personal journey to nativelike proficiency are the most palpable. In every chapter, for example, the individual stories are broken up by graphic text boxes containing quotations from the individual learners about their language learning journeys. These quotations contribute immensely to understanding the context of the leaners and their mindset regarding their own progress in the language. Colin, for example, in Chapter 4 does not simply have an "ear for the language," as the chapter title suggests; he also has a particular way of viewing his pathway to proficiency: "You have to become somebody else. You can't stay yourself; you can't stay English if you're going to speak a foreign language. You have to give that up" (p. 78). Such glimpses into the learning process and learner perspective of each participant gives their individual stories much more context and relevance to a wider range of language learners/readers.

In the concluding remarks to *Stories from Exceptional Language Learners Who Have Achieved Nativelike Proficiency*, the authors state that they hoped to "pull back the curtain" (p. 183) on the process of achieving the highest levels of language proficiency through their interviews and learners' narratives. The volume more than succeeds in this aim. The authors have created a cohesive collection of thirty stories of success that gives the reader reason both to aspire to, but also to interrogate, nativelike proficiency. It delivers nothing less than an array of diverse, compelling portraits of successful–though not always uncontroversial–experiences in language learning. For any learner or instructor interested in attaining the highest levels of measurable proficiency in world languages and cultures, this volume is an exciting collection of case studies and varied experiences that can only add to our understanding of attaining this desirable, though elusive, goal.

About the Reviewer

Thomas Jesús Garza (EdD Harvard University) is Associate Professor in the Department of Slavic and Eurasian Studies and founding Director of the College of Liberal Arts Texas Language Center at the University of Texas at Austin. He has published articles in *Modern Language Journal, Foreign Language Annuals, Slavic and East European Journal, Russian Language Journal,* and *Current History*. He recently completed a book manuscript on filmic portraits of *machismo* in contemporary Russian and Mexican cultures and is currently working on a new project on Russian actor and bard Vladimir Vysotsky in the Americas in the 1970s.

IN MEMORIAM

In Memoriam
Professor Zoltán Dörnyei
June 10, 2022

It is with great sadness that we pass on the news of the death of our friend and colleague, Professor Zoltán Dörnyei, who died after an illness on Friday 10, June 2022. He will be greatly missed by his family, friends, and all of us in the School of English.

Zoltán began as a language teacher for International House in Budapest, before completing his PhD in Psycholinguistics at Eötvös Loránd University in 1989 with the thesis, "Psycholinguistic factors in foreign language learning." He began teaching in the School of English and American Studies at Eötvös Loránd University in 1988. A decade later, he moved to the United Kingdom, working first at Thames Valley University, London, and then joining the School of English at the University of Nottingham in 2000. In 2003 he received a DSc. in Linguistics from the Hungarian Academy of Sciences. In 2017 Zoltán also completed a second PhD, this time in Theology from Durham University with the thesis, "Progressive creation and the struggles of humankind in the Bible: an experiment in canonical narrative interpretation." He became Professor of Psycholinguistics in 2004.

In the School of English, Zoltán's work focused on how motivation affects the language learning process. As a lecturer, he taught modules explaining language learning and teaching English as a second language for undergraduate and postgraduate students. He also regularly conducted teacher training seminars and workshops, and he spoke at many conferences for language teachers. He was the author of numerous books on language learning, Christian theology and research methods. His 2007 book, *Research Methods in Applied Linguistics: Quantitative, Qualitative and Mixed Methodologies*, is widely regarded as the key manual in the field. His applied linguistics books encompassed discipline-defining work as well as hands-on practical guides for teachers and fellow researchers. Zoltán was also regarded as a significant theologian and writer on the Christian life. His 2013 co-edited collection, *Christian Faith and English Language Teaching and Learning*, brought together the two sides of his thinking.

We have received a great number of messages of condolence from many former students of Zoltán's recalling fond memories of inspirational lectures, kind and wise mentorship, and encouragement towards their own intellectual rigor. His legacy will remain not only in the major body of published work that he leaves for future scholars, but in the thousands of teachers worldwide he has influenced, and the language classrooms that have been changed under his inspiration. It is remarkable to witness the respect, admiration, and love not only from his many former doctoral students but also from those who never met him yet were touched by his influence. This reach across the world will ensure that the spirit of his work will long endure.

... [His] funeral [was] livestreamed on YouTube: https://www.youtube.com/watch?v=tQajO0VMA5M

Posted on Monday 13th June 2022 at the website of the University of Nottingham

In Memoriam
Carl D. Leaver
1948-2021

It is with great sadness that MSI Press notes the loss of Carl Don Leaver, co-founder of the Press and typesetter and graphic designer *par excellence*. Many authors have expressed not only condolences but also a sense of legacy from covers he designed that they love. He designed and typeset the *Journal for Distinguished Language Studies* from its initial volume, and the journal's cover design has been retained through the current issue.

On August 16, 2021, Carl Leaver of San Juan Bautista, California passed into eternal rest. A forester with the US Forest Service in Idaho and Montana, he turned to nature photography while working in the Bitterroot National Forest. His photographs graced national magazine covers and on a weekly basis the local paper of Hamilton, MT, the *Ravalli Republican*. He later worked on photography projects for the US Army (AFEES) and taught photography at the New York Institute of Technology in Amman, Jordan. His final career change led him to computer graphics and publishing; his many typeset books and book covers have helped MSI Press authors win a large number of awards over the years, and MSI Press has been rated in several categories as one of the top publishers in California, thanks in part to his skill at typesetting and graphics.

As a memorial to Carl, MSI Press is now hosting a web page, Carl's Cancer Consortium (CCC), at the MSI Press website. The CCC is a one-stop starting point for all things cancer, to make it easier for those with cancer to find answers to questions that can otherwise take hours to track down on the Internet and/or from professionals, taking precious time away from being present to the relative, friend, or self with cancer.

Citation at Carl Leaver's memorial service:

"To laugh often and much; to win the respect of intelligent people and the affection of children...to leave the world a better place...to know even one life has breathed easier because you have lived. This is to have succeeded." - Ralph Waldo Emerson

Posted on MSI Press blog August 16, 2021

LIST OF CONTRIBUTORS
TO THIS VOLUME

James Bernhardt
Gerd Brendel

Emilie Cleret
Jérôme Collin
Andrew Corin

Tanya de Hoyos

Sergey Entis

Joseph Fees
Jack Franke

Thomas Jesús Garza

Francesca Gasparella

Irene Krasner
Cornelius Kubler

Betty Lou Leaver
Natalia Lord

Alessandra Rice

Michael Wei

Yalun Zhou

CALL FOR PAPERS

Journal for Distinguished Language Studies
Volume 9, 2023-2024
A refereed journal

Overview

The *Journal for Distinguished Language Studies* (JDLS), founded by the Coalition of Distinguished Language Centers under the direction of Dr. Betty Lou Leaver and Boris Shekhtman in 2002, is a refereed volume and the only journal to focus exclusively on the highest levels of language achievement, that is, native-like or near-native. This level is labeled *Distinguished* by the American Council on the Teaching of Foreign Languages (ACTFL), *Level 4/Advanced Professional Proficiency* by the Interagency Language Roundtable (ILR), and also Level 4 as part of the Standardized Agreement (STANAG) 6001 of NATO's Bureau of International Language Co-ordination (BILC). Descriptions can be found at the ACTFL, ILR, and BILC websites.

The purpose of this journal is to create a robust international movement to promote and support language learning to the near-native level of proficiency. The editors are seeking contributions in the areas of theory, research, and applications. The journal typically has published a balance of articles in all three categories. Published papers will thus develop theory, share applications that work (based on the experience of those who teach that level), and report on the research conducted and needed for proper evaluation and assessment of theory and application.

We particularly welcome articles on the following themes:

- current status of Level 4 proficiency research in each of the four skill areas;
- teaching methods to/at/above Level 4 proficiency in each of the four skill areas;
- the role of culture in achieving Level 4 proficiency in each of the four skill areas;
- assessment to/at/above Level 4 proficiency in each of the four skill areas; and
- related topics as long as they focus on Level 4.

Submissions should represent original work. They should not have been previously published elsewhere nor be currently submitted to another journal or collected volume.

Submission Process and Deadlines

1. Articles are accepted on a rolling basis; however, articles submitted after June 30, 2024 must first receive permission from one of the editors.
2. Please submit (5,000-8,000 Word doc.) articles no later June 30, 2024. Include paper title (10 words max.), abstract (200-250 words max.), affiliation, and one blind copy (omitting the name and institutional affiliation of the author at the beginning of the article). Blinded articles will be sent to reviewers.
3. Use *Publication Manual of the American Psychological Association*, Seventh Edition.
4. Because journal articles are now English only, please ensure that a native speaker/proficient writer proofreads prior to submission so peer review can focus on content. The editors reserve the right to return, without review, any articles that are not clear, accurate, or concise (i.e., minimum Level 4 writing proficiency).
5. We expect to receive reviewers' recommendations by September 1 (earlier for those articles submitted earlier), immediately after which we will let potential contributors know whether the manuscript has been accepted, needs revision, or has been rejected. We will need to receive revised manuscripts no later than November 15, 2024.
6. Publication is anticipated for December 31, 2024, with galleys available for proofreading in early December.
7. Potential authors can contact the editors in advance with any questions.

Request specs from/submit articles to: Dr. Yalun Zhou (zhouy12@rpi. edu)

Copy: Dr. Donna Bain Butler (dbutler@desu.edu)

AN UPDATED CALL FOR PROPOSALS, ACCEPTED ON A ROLLING BASIS, IS AVAILABLE AT
WWW.MSIPRESS.COM/JOURNAL-FOR-DISTINGUISHED-LANGUAGE-STUDIES/

www.ingramcontent.com/pod-product-compliance
Lightning Source LLC
Chambersburg PA
CBHW040739300426
44111CB00026B/2985